Violence and Reconstruction

Edited by John Darby

FROM THE
JOAN B. KROC INSTITUTE
FOR INTERNATIONAL PEACE STUDIES

THE RIREC PROJECT ON POST-ACCORD PEACE BUILDING

■

THE RESEARCH INITIATIVE ON THE RESOLUTION OF ETHNIC CONFLICT

Violence

and

Reconstruction

■ EDITED BY JOHN DARBY

UNIVERSITY OF NOTRE DAME PRESS
NOTRE DAME, INDIANA

Copyright © 2006 by the University of Notre Dame
Notre dame, Indiana 46556
www.undpress.nd.edu
Manufactured in the United States of America

Book design by Nancy Berliner
Set in type by Berliner, Inc., New York, New York

Library of Congress Cataloging-in-Publication Data

Violence and reconstruction / edited by John Darby.
   p. cm.
  "The RIREC Project on Post-Accord Peace Building"—
  "One of three edited volumes resulting from a three-year collaborative Research Initiative on the Resolution of Ethnic Conflict (RIREC) at the Joan B. Kroc Institute for International Peace Studies at the University of Notre Dame"—Pref.
  Includes bibliographical references and index.
  ISBN 0-268-02587-8 (cloth : alk. paper)
  ISBN 0-268-02588-6 (pbk. : alk. paper)
  1. Political violence. 2. Postwar reconstruction. 3. Peace-building. I. Darby, John (John P.)
II. RIREC Project on Post-Accord Peace Building.
  JC328.6.V553 2005
  303.6'2—dc22

                            2005021177

CONTENTS

Acknowledgments

This book arises from a research project funded by and based in the Joan B. Kroc Institute for International Peace Studies at the University of Notre Dame, and I am grateful for the support of the institute and of my colleagues there. I particularly appreciate the advice and guidance of Tristan Anne Borer and Siobhán McEvoy-Levy, with whom this project was conceived and developed, and Rashied Omar, who helped us carry it through. My interest in the effects of violence on peace processes began while I was a Jennings Randolph Fellow at the United States Institute of Peace and developed while I was a Fulbright New Century Scholar in 2003. I am grateful for responses from Scott Appleby, Sana Farid, Thomas Pettigrew, Roger Mac Ginty, Dominic Murray, Mirak Raheem, and Irene Zirimwabagabo on the final chapter. My main gratitude is for the ingenuity and patience of my fellow contributors to this book.

PREFACE

This book is one of three edited volumes resulting from a three-year collaborative Research Initiative on the Resolution of Ethnic Conflict (RIREC) at the Joan B. Kroc Institute for International Peace Studies at the University of Notre Dame. From 2000 to 2003, the RIREC initiative examined the problems and challenges that develop after a peace accord has been reached between conflicting parties but before the agreement has been fully implemented. It focused on post-accord peacebuilding and the difficult but pressing questions of how to create a sustainable just peace after a period of protracted conflict. The project set out to understand why so many recent peace accords have not been successfully implemented and to provide guidance from experience for those engaged in peace building.

The RIREC project identified and integrated the study of three key dimensions of the post-accord landscape: post-accord violence, the role of young people in violent conflict and peace building, and truth telling and peace building. A research cluster was developed for each dimension and brought together a team of interdisciplinary international scholars and practitioners for a series of workshops and an international conference at the University of Notre Dame in September 2003 on the theme of "Peacebuilding after Peace Accords."

Each research cluster resulted in an edited book. In addition to this book, the truth-telling and peace building-cluster, directed by Tristan Anne Borer, produced *Telling the Truths: Truth Telling and Peace Building in Post-Conflict Societies,* and the youth and peace-building research team, directed by Siobhán McEvoy-Levy, produced *Troublemakers and Peacemakers: Youth and Post-Accord Peace Building.*

Separately, each of these dimensions combines conflict management and conflict transformation challenges and opportunities. The synergy between youth, truth telling and transitional justice, and post-accord violence, however, has not been conceptualized in this fashion, much less systematically studied as a dynamic process generating its own outcomes and patterns of behavior. Yet any peace process is doomed to failure if it lacks a realistic strategy to reduce levels of violence and counter violence; if it skirts the hard political, legal, and cultural choices that nurture genuine reconciliation; and if it fails to recognize and accommodate the central role of youth.

Together, the series of three books develops new perspectives on post-accord peace building, as well as on the intersections between different aspects of reconstruction that were once studied in isolation.

JOHN DARBY

The Post-Accord Context

Make no mistake: we are living at a remarkable hinge of history and it's not clear how it's going to swing.

— *Thomas L. Friedman*

First, a personal admission. "In the last few years," I wrote in 1997, "a number of durable and traditional ethnic conflicts seem to be lurching along the continuum from violence towards settlement, or at least compromise" (Darby 1997, 12). In support of this contention I cited developments in South Africa, the Middle East, Northern Ireland, the Basque Country, Sri Lanka, Mozambique, El Salvador, Corsica, and even (somewhat to my later embarrassment) Chechnya.

Some of these peace processes have collapsed. Others have failed to fulfill their early promise. Even those that accomplished a peace agreement are still besieged by problems. Post-agreement redevelopment in South Africa and El Salvador has been frustrated by high crime and low economic growth. Six years after the Good Friday Agreement, Northern Ireland flounders in a no-war, no-settlement stalemate. A peace agreement is no guarantee against continuing violence. This is the subject of this book.

There is already a substantial and rapidly growing literature on the relation-ship between violence, ethnicity, and conflict resolution. A number of institutes and centers have been charting the changing patterns in contemporary violence throughout the world, and they continue to update the patterns on a regular basis.[1] As a result of these and other studies we have a much more detailed understanding of how these patterns have shifted, most notably away from inter-national wars and toward internal violence. In 2000, for example, only two of the twenty-five major conflicts listed by the Stockholm International Peace In-stitute were international conflicts. The reason for violence is disputed. The mainstream political science literature tends to explain civil conflict as arising from grievances such as economic inequality, political domination, or ethnic divisions. In what has become known as the "greed versus grievance" debate, Paul Collier and colleagues at the World Bank argue that "opportunity pro-vides considerably more explanatory power than grievance" in explaining civil wars (Collier and Hoeffler 2001, 1). Following an analysis of seventy-eight major civil conflicts between 1960 and 1999, they conclude that conditions conducive to building rebel organizations—access to finance, ability to extort natural re-sources, environments supportive of rebel groups—provide a better explanation for rebellion than grievance.

We also know more about the optimum conditions for intervention in situ-ations of violence. Doyle, Johnstone, and Orr (1997) have described the changes in multidimensional peacekeeping in Cambodia and El Salvador, primarily from a UN perspective. Hampson's (1996) study of five peace settlements, again, all cases involving UN involvement, singled out the role of third parties and empha-sized the importance of post-accord implementation. Comparative studies by Darby and Mac Ginty (2000) highlighted different approaches to five peace processes that have developed since the early 1990s, processes that were generat-ed more by internal rivals than by the UN or other international actors (Darby and Mac Ginty 2000, 2003). All of these have confirmed the central role played by violence in determining the timing and chances of success for peace initia-tives. Mediators have a better chance of success in the early stages of protracted conflicts because "attitudes and perceptions have not hardened and parties are still willing to talk with each other" (Crocker, Hampson, and Aall 2001, 26). As violence increases, it has been argued that coercion by external states may be needed to supply "the requisite political will and 'muscle' required to bring par-ties to the table and to end violence" (Crocker, Hampson, and Aall 2001, 669; see also Stedman 1997). In the main, most studies of violence and ethnic conflict have concentrated on how entry points may be found for external intervention in the conflict cycle. Zartman (1989b) and Haass (1990) emphasized the impor-tance of taking advantage of the "ripe moment" when the parties in conflict have reached a "hurting stalemate": when the costs and prospects of war outweigh the costs and prospects of settlement for the major combatants. It is still remarkable that the dominant message from research on these peace processes shows that modern wars are more likely to terminate at the negotiating table than on the battlefield (Wallensteen and Sollenberg 2001, King 1997).[2]

The potential of violence to disrupt peace processes has not been neglected. Stedman (1997) has identified the part played by spoilers—dissidents who refuse to go along when militants have gone into negotiation—in disrupting peace processes, particularly with respect to the political, economic, and security vulnerability of many states emerging from civil wars (Stedman, Rothchild, and Cousens 2002). It is not uncommon for a peace process to be overturned by violence after an accord has been agreed and is being implemented, as happened in Israel-Palestine and Angola (Hampson 1996).

VIOLENCE AND PEACE PROCESSES

There is no shortage of evidence demonstrating that violence has frequently destabilized peace processes. The peace negotiations in South Africa were almost derailed by the Boipatong massacre in 1992. The Irish Republican Army (IRA) ceasefire that started the process in Northern Ireland was terminated by the Canary Wharf bomb in 1996, which put the peace process in limbo for well over a year. In the Basque Country two ETA (Euskadi ta Askatasuna) ceasefires failed to stimulate negotiations, and violence resumed in 1999 at a higher level than before. The return of serious violence in Israel-Palestine since late 2000 has at best seriously disrupted the Oslo process and at worst ended it. Every attempt to end the wars in Colombia since the 1998 Pastrana initiative has foundered as a result of pernicious violence.

The effects of violence are not universal or constant. They vary among different settings and among different stages in the peace process in each setting. Peace processes are often regarded as following preordained stages: first, prenegotiation, often involving secret talks, during which the terms of disengagement from violence and engagement in negotiations are agreed upon; then the formal ending of violence, usually through ceasefires; next the negotiations themselves, aiming at producing a formal agreement; and finally, what is often referred to as post-settlement peace building or reconstruction. Violence affects each of these phases differently. Although a peace process usually follows open warfare between a highly militarized state and guerrilla-type opposition, the level of violence may intensify during the prenegotiation phase as combatants try to optimize their negotiating positions. The negotiations themselves are often accompanied by the emergence of more extreme dissident groups. Negotiators also have to confront a new range of priority issues, including demands for the early release of prisoners, demobilization and disarmament,[3] and policing reform, as well as the reintegration of militants into society and consideration of their victims. Although these patterns generally apply, they are also heavily influenced by local distinctions. In Northern Ireland the decommissioning of weapons became one of the most formidable obstacles after the Good Friday Agreement, yet it was bypassed at a brisk trot in South Africa. A peace process is rarely a predictable sequence from violence to settlement.

Even when political violence is ended by the declaration of a ceasefire, violence may continue from three different sources. To complicate matters further, a number of new violence-related issues will emerge to challenge the negotiations.[4]

VIOLENCE BY THE STATE

Governments are often as divided as their opponents about entering negotiations. Those responsible for security are often more skeptical than their political leaders about why militants enter negotiations. In Guatemala and East Timor, state violence continued after ceasefires and even after agreements. Governments or quasi-governmental agencies continue covert actions either to strengthen their position going into negotiations or to influence the outcome. Even if such pressure is not applied, the security apparatus built up during periods of violence becomes a potential danger when they end. The size of the army and police force, augmented during the war, is likely to be diminished, endangering jobs and personal security. Demands are made to reform the police force that regarded itself as the bastion against terrorism. Unless handled carefully, disaffection within the security forces has the potential to undermine the peace process itself.

VIOLENCE FROM MILITANTS

The declaration of a ceasefire by militants is never unanimous, and its continuation is contingent on achieving concrete rewards during the subsequent negotiations, such as early prisoner releases and the dismantling of the state's security apparatus. These rewards are rarely immediate. Consequently, the pendulum may swing back toward the militants who opposed negotiations in the first place.

The most obvious threat is that the ex-militants who have entered negotiations will abandon them and return to political violence, as happened during negotiations in Northern Ireland and South Africa. For some of their colleagues, the agreement to enter into talks implies that the purity of their cause has been betrayed. The result is often a rise in violence from splinter groups determined to continue the armed struggle. Indeed, it is difficult to find a move toward negotiations unaccompanied by a split between ideological zealots and the dealers who enter into talks. Even those who have entered negotiations may seek to use tactical violence to advance their aims around the conference table. In addition, the struggle for control among ex-militants may lead to dangerous and vicious turf wars. Violence between factions within the Palestinian community, for example, grew after the first transfer of land to Palestinian control in 1995. Punishment beatings persisted in Northern Ireland after the Good Friday Agreement as both loyalists and republicans exercised what they regarded as their policing role.

VIOLENCE ON THE GROUND

The relaxation of paramilitary discipline that follows a peace agreement carries its own dangers. The underlying hatred remains, often taking the form of riots and undisciplined confrontations with ethnic rivals or the security forces. In Northern Ireland the declaration of the ceasefires, and the ending of direct violence between organized paramilitaries and the security forces, was marked by a return to more direct violence between Catholics and Protestants, especially during the annual marching seasons. This can threaten a peace process by drawing back into violence those militants who may have entered negotiations but have not divorced themselves from the instincts and antagonisms of their communities.

In addition to growing confrontational violence, the level of conventional crime, especially violent crime, is also likely to rise after a peace agreement, fueled by the arms stockpiled during the years of violence. In 1996 there was at least one firearm in 20 percent of South African households. In Angola an AK-47 could be bought for the price of a chicken (Naylor 1997). The criminal aspects of paramilitary campaigns often transmute into crime syndicates, particularly those involving drug smuggling and dealing. The security services, more geared toward political than conventional crime during the war years, are often ill equipped to deal with them. Underlying all of this, people have become accustomed to routine violence. Expectations of immediate economic and other improvements, raised during the period of negotiations, are often disappointed after the accord is signed.

Violence from any of these three sources may threaten peace processes. In addition, when a ceasefire is declared and negotiations start, a number of new security-related issues that are not negotiable during the war suddenly demand immediate attention. Three of the most common are the early release of political prisoners, demobilization and disarmament, and reform of the police and the security forces. Even if a general agreement is reached, negotiations on these issues can run on for years, and they frequently fail.

POST-ACCORD VIOLENCE

Although substantial research attention has been paid to the origins and dynamics of ethnic violence, to the first moves toward negotiations, and to spoiler violence, the threat to post-accord reconstruction is under-researched.[5] Yet the signing of a multiparty peace accord is unlikely to end violence. Indeed, just as the forms of violence are transmuted at the start of peace processes, the emphasis often changes again during post-accord implementation.

There is ample evidence that state violence may continue even after peace accords are signed. According to South Africa's Minister of Safety and Security, some members of both the state security services and the African National Congress (ANC) were still active in crime syndicates as late as 1998 (Republic of South Africa 1998). In Indonesia the inability or unwillingness of the government to control the actions of its security forces in East Timor in the buildup to the independence referendum in 1999 led to many deaths and the forced evacuation of 200,000 people. In the face of considerable international pressure, the foreign minister, Ali Alatas, eventually admitted that military and police had participated in the violence, but he attributed it to "rogue elements" and "criminal activities."[6] Since then a report commissioned by the United Nations concluded that, far from a few soldiers misbehaving, a systematic campaign of terror had been "planned and carried out" by the Indonesian army, with militia participation, to undermine the vote for independence in the referendum. The report concluded: "Several of the senior officers named in this report not only sponsored the setting up of the militia, providing training, arms, money and in some cases drugs; they also encouraged its campaign of violence and organized the wave of destruction and deportation that occurred between 5 and 20 September [1999]."[7]

The tendency for militant organizations to fragment during negotiations has already been noted. This increases in intensity if the leaders agree to sign a peace accord. After the Good Friday Agreement in Northern Ireland, groups like the "Real" IRA and the Continuity IRA picked up the torch they believed had been surrendered by Sinn Féin. The Oslo accords in Israel-Palestine were followed by Palestinian attempts to bomb them away; the killing of twenty-eight Muslims by the Israeli settler Baruch Goldstein in 1994 and the assassination of the Israeli prime minister Yitzhak Rabin in 1995 showed that zealots from both communities were eager to overturn the process.

Even if zealots are unable to sustain a violent campaign, the postwar years may experience an increase in direct confrontations between ethnic rivals and a rise in conventional crime. By 1998 violent crime emerged as the most serious problem in both Guatemala and San Salvador, raising concern about a possible correlation between high crime rates and disrespect for new democratic institutions. During the 1990s the crime rate rose to such a degree in South Africa that it seriously undermined post-settlement peace building. It undermined inward investment, tourism, and general confidence in the new government. By the mid-1990s the high level of conventional crime had far outpaced political violence as a destabilizing factor. By 1998 the daily homicide rate was sixty-eight (Du Toit 2001, 98), the world's highest murder rate. It was not helped by low conviction rates (Sidiropoulos 1998, 58). More ominously, the barrier between ordinary crime and South Africa's underlying racial tensions, never sharp, became increasingly blurred. Fifteen hundred white farmers were attacked between 1994 and 1998, resulting in more than two hundred murders, which threatened to create a loop back from post-settlement civil violence to the violence familiar from the earlier struggle. In Northern Ireland the number of violent crimes fell between the 1994 ceasefires and the Good Friday Agreement, but they rose by 21.2 percent in the two years following the accord (Police Authority 1999, 58 and 63), although it is difficult to distinguish the specific causes of the rise.

Violence may also threaten peace processes through the contentious security-related issues they raise. Most of these—early release of political prisoners, decommissioning of illegal weapons, and reform of the police and the security forces—are implemented only after an agreement has been signed, although discussions on prisoner release often start even before negotiations begin. Indeed, the South African peace process actually began with the release of prisoners when Nelson Mandela and other ANC leaders were set free in February 1990. Even if the principle of early prisoner release is accepted, and the terms for release are agreed, the actual releases are usually deferred until a general accord has been signed, thereby running the risk of increasing public hostility to the agreement itself. The rate of prisoner releases has been a constant source of bitter dispute in Israel-Palestine, but it was implemented relatively smoothly in Northern Ireland. Decommissioning of weapons is a more complicated matter. The 1991 South African National Peace Accord did not ask the ANC to disband paramilitary units nor hand over their arms caches; it required only that firearms not be displayed at public meetings. However, failure to reach agreement on the decommissioning of paramilitary weapons continued to undermine the Good Friday Agreement in Northern Ireland for many years. Police reform is an equally emotive issue in negotiations. It is axiomatic that divided societies require a police force that reflects the divisions. Section 195 of the 1996

South African constitution, for example, insisted that the police and defense forces "be broadly representative of the South African people." Stanley and Call (2003) have suggested that two broad strategies are available to accomplish this objective: integration of ex-militants into the police force or structural reform of the force.

THE APPROACH

Peace processes are the consequence of violence, and violence seriously affects their direction. It continues to determine their outcome even after a peace accord has been reached. The aim of this book is to explore analytically the different ways that violence can influence the implementation of peace agreements and postwar reconstruction.

The main framework for analysis is constructed around the actors using violence. Kristine Höglund and I. William Zartman consider how state violence alters during this phase of peacemaking. Marie-Joëlle Zahar develops the debate on spoiler violence. The effects of other forms of violence, including conventional nonpolitical crime, are analyzed by Roger Mac Ginty. Demilitarization, decommissioning, and reintegration are the subject of Virginia Gamba's chapter, and Dominic Murray reviews options for policing reform. Timothy Sisk's theme is the potential provided by violence for positive change. Each of these chapters raises and addresses important questions about how these different forms of violence may be managed in the pursuit of a just and enduring peace.

NOTES

1. See, for example, Gurr (2001) and Geller and Singer (1998). Sollenberg and Wallensteen's (2001) states in armed conflict and the *World Conflict Map* produced by PIOMM (The International Research Program on Causes of Human Rights Violation) (1997) is updated regularly, as is Crisis Watch (www.crisisweb.org). The epigraph for this chapter is taken from Thomas L. Friedman, "War of Ideas: Part 2," *New York Times,* January 11, 2004.

2. For a similar finding, see also Marshall and Gurr (2003).

3. There is a growing literature on demobilization, disarmament, and reconstruction (DDR). "Demobilization" usually refers to the reduction or removal of arms held by state agents, the army, or the police, and the term "disarmament" is used to describe the handing over of weapons held by militants. These common usages are somewhat complicated by the popular usage of "decommissioning" in Northern Ireland to describe disarmament by paramilitary organizations.

4. For a more detailed description of this analysis, see Darby (2001).

5. A notable exception is Stedman, Rothchild, and Cousens (2002). In *Ending Civil Wars: The Implementation of Peace Agreements,* they have carried the analysis into post-settlement peace building and pointed to the difficulties facing post-accord states in providing economic regeneration and security and in rebuilding civil society.

6. *New York Times,* September 10, 1999.

7. "East Timor Massacre Work of Indonesia's Army," *Sydney Morning Herald,* April 20, 2001.

KRISTINE HÖGLUND AND I. WILLIAM ZARTMAN

Violence by the State

Official Spoilers and Their Allies

Parties in a conflict usually pursue both a conflict track and a settlement track at the same time, one of them dominant but the other never fully absent until a final decision has been made, and maybe not even then (Zartman 1989b). If agreements are made by factions on both sides looking for an end to conflict, the implication is that both sides will have to carry along recalcitrant parties, opponents of settlement, and spoilers, who can be expected to continue the path of violence during the negotiations.[1] Within the state, the actor with which this chapter is concerned, these negative forces can come from three elements: the military, whose job it is to fight; militias, whose job it is to pursue conflict behaviors that the state cannot; and decision makers, who tend the conflict track until it is completely replaced by the settlement track. In studies of negotiation and peace processes, it is the behavior of the dominant current in each party that is usually analyzed, and parties are assumed to be homogeneous. The role of the opponents of peace processes is not often studied and needs more attention. As a result of the motivational uncertainty of the main sources, the interesting question for practitioners and analysts alike is whether their conflict behavior during the settlement process is tactical and positive in regard to the process or destabilizing and negative, and in either case how it can be handled to promote settlement.

The same elements are present in the early post-agreement period, until the agreement fully takes hold and eliminates any possibility of reopening the conflict. These elements continue after the decision to end conflict out of habit and predilection, in the first case simply by continuing their past actions but in the second by continuing their past policies even when they are no longer officially sanctioned. However, conflict continuation may also be officially sanctioned when the main decision makers do not believe that the decision was correct for them or that their opponents will hold to it. The other side needs to be considered and brought into the settlement politics, for in the process of implementing the agreement it can turn back to violence, either to destabilize the agreement or to dominate the post-agreement evolution of the system. Here the interesting questions are whether the violent behavior after settlement is residual or intentional (neither of them very positive for the peace process) and how it can brought under control.

In both cases, a key to understanding how violence can be managed and brought under control is to consider its varying effects on the dynamics of peace making. State violence can have an important effect on the parties' choice to pursue a negotiated settlement and its implementation because it influences the decision makers' considerations both about the consequences of continued armed conflict and about the costs associated with peace. Concerned third parties will have to take both of these factors into consideration when evaluating strategies to deal with spoilers.

This chapter will examine the role of state spoilers and violence in peace processes, leaving aside the similar role on the other side of the conflict.[2] The state side operates under a greater presumption of coherence, control, and homogeneity, so that state spoilers may be considered a more unusual and therefore interesting phenomenon. However, as noted, an assumption about state homogeneity is often oversimplified and misleading since it does not take into account the power struggles within a state that can impede attempts to solve the conflict. Moreover, state violence is particularly interesting to consider because the state will hold on to some kind of legitimate use of force both during the negotiations and in the post-accord period. This means that the state has to retain some capacity of violence for security and civilian policing, while the rebel group will have to disarm and demobilize or be integrated into the state structures. The subject will be examined from the point of view of the peace process, with the aim of explaining why the spoiler operates and how violence can be brought under control.

We use the term "state spoiler" to indicate the destructive use of violence by the state actor or elements associated with the state.[3] While Stedman has argued that spoilers only exist when there is something to spoil—that is, "when a comprehensive peace agreement has been signed or when at least two of the adversaries have committed themselves publicly to a pact" (Stedman 1997, 7)—the adopted view in this chapter is that spoilers can be present once a peace process is set in motion and a negotiated settlement comes into sight. While bringing down a peace process is one of the purposes of the use of violence, in this chapter we argue that violence is used for many purposes, such as pacifying critics within the group or putting pressure on the other side to make concessions in the negotiations.

BRINGING THE STATE AND ITS ALLIES INTO AN AGREEMENT

The decision to pursue a conflict is generally (one may say, universally) preceded by debate between those in favor and those against; once that decision is made, the debate usually (one may even say, generally) continues in some form, the parties tending to pursue both the conflict and the settlement track in varying proportions. The same mixture is present when the decision to switch to the settlement track is finally made. That shift, discussed further below, is a major political event, not only because of its substantive implications but also procedurally, because it means turning off the public support for a conflict that has been a major political and emotional investment and turning on similar support for settlement, with its implications of peace and reconciliation with the former enemy. Even when sincerely engaged on the road to settlement, parties tend to keep the conflict track alive, both as an insurance policy in case of failure on the settlement track and as a reinforcement policy to strengthen their hand in the settlement negotiations.

But there will also be those who keep the conflict track alive because it remains for them the preferred course of action—hangovers from the previous policy mix who opposed the shift to settlement as the upper track. While these may still be tactically useful to the "settlers," as noted, they resent their instrumental role and would prefer to have the conflict option continue to occupy the upper track. Thus, their aim becomes not only to pursue the erstwhile preferred policy out of nostalgia but also to undermine the newly preferred policy of settlement. Their target becomes both the enemy and the new policy of their own government.

In unusual situations, it may even be the government that favors staying the conflict course even while ostensibly pursuing settlement. It may be engaged in negotiations because of external pressure, or to obtain a lull in the fighting in order to rearm, or as an internal tactical calculation to show up the opponent; if the rebels agree to the government's settlement terms, then a settlement is reached, but the latter remains skeptical about such a possibility. In this case, the pursuit of conflict is no contradiction but rather the maintenance of a course that fits either eventuality dictated by the opponent's policy choice.

Maintenance of the conflict track after a decision to pursue settlement can come from three main elements: the military, militias, and decision makers discontent with the turn to a settlement track. The effectiveness of each in pursuing its conflict behavior depends on their operational autonomy; parties that regret the shift to the settlement track but cannot do anything about it merely sit and pout.

The military is the official agent of conflict and is in large part unemployed when conflict is over. Thus, members of the military and the security forces, who consider themselves as having protected the state during the war, may be ideologically disillusioned by the fact that the cause is being compromised or because they are being sidelined during the negotiations (Darby 2001). Moreover, settlement often means a loss by the politicians of some of the gains made by the military, calling into question the whole field of civil-military relations; for example, military coups frequently occur when politicians undo military accomplishments or produce military defeats. In addition, even while settlement negotiations are going on, the military maintains its mission and remains responsible for the security of the country and the preservation of its position of strength as a basis for negotiation. If a ceasefire has already been obtained, this mission still requires a high state of alert to make sure that it is observed by the other side; when a ceasefire itself is a subject of negotiations, the military must pursue the conflict until there is a ceasefire but in such a way as to not upset the settlement track. There is so much delicacy in these conflicting aspects of the military's position that conflict continuation is as likely as conflict containment, with important consequences for the incipient settlement track. Beyond these side effects of their legitimate job, the military may also be making money out of the conflict through sideline activities related to procurement, occupation, protection, etc. Indeed, in many cases the military develops close ties with organized crime.

"Militias," a term used here to include prostate paramilitary groups, are in an even more difficult situation with regard to settlement. Not only are they, like the army, unemployed (at least in officially approved tasks) under ceasefires and settlements, but they are under much less direct and effective control by the politicians involved in the settlement track. Militias, therefore, have the greatest degree of operational autonomy. They face all the mission-related temptations of the army, with no guaranteed role after settlement. Their irregularity, assured under conflict, has no cover under peace. Furthermore, they tend to have special ties with parts of the decision-making elite, the very parts that are most likely to have opposed adoption of the settlement track in the first place. Then, too, the militia is even more likely than the military to profit from sideline activities under the cover of the conflict.

Politicians on the conflict track have whatever autonomy their position gives them, but they are not themselves perpetrators of violence; they need to get others to do the job. Their range of roles is large, spanning from sincere "settlers" manipulating violence for tactical purposes to sincere spoilers out to torpedo the peace talks. The real—as opposed to the good—reasons for their position also vary, ranging from a conviction of what is best for their country in terms of the conflict to a conviction of what is best for themselves in terms of its spoils. Because of these ranges, it is harder to establish with certainty the type of spoiler in question. Yet determining the motive is crucial to determining the appropriate measures of control. Particularly delicate is the rupture of ceasefires during negotiations—are ruptures a negative or a positive move? Hamas's de facto breach of the Road Map ceasefire in early August 2003 with a suicide bombing and de jure breach with a formal announcement after Israel continued to apply terror and assassination in Gaza and the West Bank is a salient case. So is Nepal in the same period: "Observers in Nepal were divided over whether the Maoists were bluffing or serious about resuming hostilities.... 'It's very ambiguous, the way it is written,' said Kunda Dixit, editor of *The Nepali Times,* referring to the Maoists' statement. 'Some people have analyzed that it's off. Some people have said that it's a way to put more pressure.'"[4]

BRINGING THE STATE AND ITS ALLIES INTO IMPLEMENTATION OF AN AGREEMENT

Once the settlement agreement is signed and hostilities are officially ended—whether the ceasefire preceded or accompanied the agreement—the remnants of the two policy tracks remain, as do old habits and missions, until the agreement fully takes hold and eliminates any possibility of reopening the conflict. The side that advocated violence was the loser in the policy debate but may still be around in policy circles or outside. These people will monitor the ensuing situation carefully to check for slippage and vindication of their policy predilections, ready to jump at any leftover violence on the rebels' part to respond in kind and discredit the settlement policy. Those who conducted the violence still have their mission, with a new focus; they are not out of the picture but are still charged with security and protection of state and society and controlling any recurrence of violence.

However, conflict continuation may also be government policy when the main decision makers do not agree with the decision or do not believe that the rebels will hold to it. The ostensible "settler" track may be a conflict track in disguise, aiming to show that settlement is untenable or to use it as a Trojan horse to disarm and eliminate the rebels as before. Usually in this case, state violence is less likely to continue than to reemerge after a period of relative quiet; the peace agreement, apparently in force for a moment, breaks down. It is easy for an uncommitted government to find a pretext—or perhaps even a solid reason—for return to violence in some aspects of the rebels' behavior. The rebels need to be brought into the political system and in the process may slip back into violence, either to destabilize the agreement from their side or to dominate the post-agreement evolution of the system. Thus, even an uncommitted government will try to put the onus of return to violence on the rebels.

The same agents—military, militias, politicians—can be involved in this type of conflict behavior. The military may continue violence after settlement for the same reasons as before: either to continue the war despite government settlement policy or as part of its normal security functions. In the first case, it is in open conflict with government policy, whereas in the second it is merely doing its duty. The first is a political act, the second a military one, although the sharp conceptual distinction can easily blur in reality. The first is more difficult to bring under control since the military may be acting for its own political reasons, as part of the original conflict track of decision makers, or for its own socioeconomic reasons, as beneficiaries from the conflict. Ordering them back in line may be insufficient; they may have to be paid or bought off in some way. Peace agreements today usually involve some stipulations regarding the reformation of police and military, including reducing the budget and size of the forces. Of special concern is the dismantling of violence makers in the security apparatus with a reputation of being particularly brutal, often special military units such as the Estado Mayor Presidencial (EMP, presidential military guard) in Guatemala and the Koevoet in South Africa, the notorious counterinsurgency unit that operated out of Namibia. These are exactly the hard-line security agents most likely to resist a peace agreement.

Similarly, militias are the most likely to continue the conflict, for the same reasons more strongly felt. A return to normal life means a change of life for them; specifically, they have to reconvert to a political party if they are going to play the political role they fought for, much as the rebels have to do, or convert to businessmen if they are going to be able to continue their economic activities. Such conversions mean entering into the legal, political, and economic systems, quite contrary to their previous status, again posing the same types of problems as the rebels face; the rebels, however, doubtless made provision for their future status in the settlement agreement, whereas the militias are much less likely to have been part of the settlement. Because they always were outside the legal system, militias are notoriously difficult to control. So-called Ninjas, Cobras, and Zulus in Congo-Brazzaville, Legitimate Defense Groups in Algeria, and Self-Defense Units in Colombia are examples of such militias.

As before, politicians on the conflict track may be effective spoilers politically, but their operational effectiveness depends on their ability to team up with either the military or the militias. They can either be acting unofficially, as continuing opponents of government policy, or officially, as uncommitted signatories of the settlement agreement; the latter are more likely than the former to be able to enlist the support of the military or militias. Official spoilers are the most difficult to control, of course, since they are in charge of the control mechanism. In determining whether official spoilers are reacting to bad faith on the other side or simply pursuing their own conflict track, it is important to interpret what they say in light of what they have said in the past and not be misled by contrived rationalistic inductions or confuse counterfactual conclusions with counterfactual data (Kydd and Walter 2002).

With the decision to end the armed conflict formally through a peace agreement, the driving forces behind the violence partially change, making the motives and causes more difficult to detect. The end of armed conflict does not mean the end of political conflict. Instead, transitions to peace take place in a context of a whole range of social conflicts, partially but not fully related to the conflict between the rebels and the government. In the absence of open combat, other conflicts come to the forefront that have the potential to impinge on the implementation of the peace settlement. In particular, the nature of violence is likely to change when its focus shifts from winning the war to the distribution of the spoils of peace.

In addition, once the armed conflict ends, the unity developed in the struggle soon breaks down, a phenomenon similar to the breakdown of the "funnel phase" of the anticolonial struggle once the unifying goal of independence has been achieved (Zartman 1980). Alliances dissolve and new relationships in a negotiated transition can be forged between old enemies. Hardliners from the state and the armed opposition can become partners in rejection, stirring so much resentment into each others' communities that each side will refuse to sit down with the other side. Atlas and Licklider point to the psychological aspects of this process. When the conflict ends and the dividing line between "us" and "them" starts to unravel, the individuals in the groups become more "cognitively aware of their differences and conflicting interests" (Atlas and Licklider 1999, 51). Attitudes toward violence and characterization of it as criminal or political also change in transitional and post-accord societies, making it more difficult to distinguish between ordinary crime and spoilers. During the war, the boundaries of political and criminal activity become obscured. The state plays a key role in this process because the state itself is often a significant source of crime (Shaw 2002). While many societies have experienced a dramatic increase in criminal violence after the signing of a peace agreement, it is often difficult to distinguish to what extent this is a continuation of violent practices from the war or a new phenomenon.

THE CONSEQUENCES OF STATE VIOLENCE

What effect does violence by the state and its allies have on the progression of a peace process? Why is it that state violence sometimes has a damaging effect on the peace talks and the implementation of a peace agreement, while at other times it has a constructive effect that speeds up the negotiation process and consolidation of peace?

Violence has a powerful effect on negotiations and their progression toward success or failure because it influences two dimensions that decision makers take into consideration when making choices to pursue a conflict track or a settlement track: the consequences of continued armed conflict (or fear of war) and the consequences of a negotiated settlement (or fear of peace). An important strategic rethink toward negotiation comes about when the two factors point the decision makers in the same direction. Fears of further negative experiences, combined with expectations of positive goals, provide the parties with the incentives to seek a negotiated settlement (Ohlson and Stedman 1994; Stedman 1996; Zartman 1989a; Ohlson 1998).

Taking these two factors into consideration, state violence can have two different effects on a negotiation process, with opposing results for its progression toward success. State violence can influence the opposing side's fears of continued conflict, making it more determined in its attempts to pursue peace. With this use, violence can directly accelerate negotiations and the implementation of a peace agreement. Indirectly, violence by the state and its allies can have a reverse effect by raising opposition to violence and influencing public opinion in favor of the peace process.

But state violence can also have the contrary effect on conflict resolution: it can increase the rebels' fears of a prospective peace settlement with the government. Violence can make the parties less willing to pursue a settlement track since it increases mistrust and raises internal divisions within a party. A direct consequence of this fear of peace is the suspension or withdrawal from negotiations or implementation of the peace agreement. In a less direct manner, violence can destabilize the new post-accord order by creating disillusionment and increasing opposition to the settlement track. In a context in which the government loses its legitimacy due to violence, peace is difficult to consolidate. Hard-line governments may come to power. Long-term peace-building and development dividends can be inhibited if violence prevents the economy from taking off.

For those involved in peace making, it can be difficult to know when violence by the other party should be taken as a lack of commitment to peace or when it is merely a bargaining tool. As noted, violence can function as a security vault, something to fall back on in case the peace process fails. In addition, to support violence, tacitly or officially, may be the only strategy available for the state actor trying to retain support from those factions most frustrated with the negotiations. A number of cases illustrate this problem. These cases are cited as examples, with no claim to representative sampling or a fortiori to any comprehensive listing. They are significant not for their statistical weight and numbers but because of their illustrative importance in the world of conflict management.

THE ANGOLAN-NAMIBIAN NEGOTIATIONS

The Angolan-Namibian negotiations of 1977–88 were replete with examples of violence during peace talks, illustrating both the positive and the negative use of violence by a bundle of actors—military, militia, and political authorities (Zartman 1989b, chap. 5). In all instances, violence was used as an instrument of official policy rather than an internally disruptive action designed to counter an official reconciliation track. While there were clearly factional differences within both composite sides—the South African government, including the South African Defense Force (SADF) and the National Union for the Total Independence of Angola (UNITA), versus the Angolan government, including the Angolan armed forces, the Cuban government and military, the South-West African Peoples Organization (SWAPO), and the Peoples Liberation Army of Namibia (PLAN)—the military actions were the collective policy decisions of each side (Crocker 1992). The evolving strategy of the South African-UNITA side was to keep both the military-political development track for Namibia and Angola and the negotiation track alive in tandem until the two tracks could meet, producing an independent Namibia friendly to South Africa and an Angola free of Cuban troops. The strategy of the Angolan-Cuban-SWAPO side was to bring about the independence of Namibia, with the concomitant withdrawal of South African forces, and the defeat of UNITA. Negotiations were mediated by the U.S.-led Contact group in the Carter administration and by the United States alone under Reagan.

Four important instances provide illustrative examples of varying calculated uses of violence during negotiations. A year after the initiation of the Contact group process, in May 1978, as the mediators formulated a general package for agreement and South Africa indicated its acceptance, the SADF launched the first major cross-border offensive against SWAPO bases at Cassinga in Angola. To SADF's surprise, SWAPO continued negotiations (despite momentary announcements to the contrary) and under Angolan pressure accepted the package in July. South Africa found it could not accept SWAPO's agreement and withdrew its own acceptance. While the Cassinga raid may be construed as an attempt to strengthen South Africa's bargaining position, the subsequent events showed instead that it was intended to provoke SWAPO into breaking off negotiations. When SWAPO did not accept the gauntlet, South Africa was obliged to pick up the spoiler role itself.

At the end of the Contact group period, while awaiting the U.S. elections, the negotiations bogged down in details, new issues, political consolidations, and diplomatic maneuvering on both sides. They were never broken off, but as they made some progress on one set of issues, other elements arose to crowd the agenda. In March 1979 and June 1980, South Africa launched major offensives: "These moves kept the first [military-political] track abreast of developments on the second [diplomatic track], a matter of greater importance for South Africa than a firm outcome on either track" (Zartman 1989b, 205). Again, in the middle of the Reagan administration mediation, when the moment appeared ripe and movement seemed promising in May 1985, Angolan troops caught a SADF commando preparing to blow up Gulf oil storage tanks in Cabinda, at a time when the United States was trying to put pressure on Angola to make a wholehearted commitment to the evolving dual-withdrawal agreement. Instead, Angola declared negotiations at an impasse, demanded an explanation from South Africa, and broke off diplomatic contacts with the U.S. mediator. South Africa provided and Angola accepted the violence as an excuse to avoid reaching the agreement for which they were not yet ready.

However, a year and a half later, the conflict escalated significantly. A major South African offensive was launched against the Angolan-UNITA base at Cuito Cuanavale and was repulsed. With Soviet approval, the number of Cuban troops was doubled and Cuba launched its own attack on the SADF in southern Angola and threatened a policy of hot pursuit, while at the same time indicating it was tired of Angola and ready to leave. South Africa cried foul, decrying Cuban violence during negotiations, but the combination of events was what produced an acceleration of movement on both sides and the eventual signature of an agreement in December 1988, providing for the withdrawal of Cuban troops from Angola and the withdrawal of South African troops from a newly independent Namibia. Violence during negotiations was the crucial element in bringing the peace process to a successful conclusion.

Israel

Israel has been a case where government violence has risen after an agreement, while in Palestine the same phenomenon has occurred at the hands of militias. There is a direct relation between the two, but one more complicated than the simple application of the Mosaic law. The Oslo Accords of September 1993 presented the negotiators with a typical reentry problem, for the secrecy with which they negotiated the agreement prevented them from preparing their publics for its signature. The reaction on both sides destroyed the Israeli pro-Oslo government: "Oslo killed Rabin, and Hamas elected Netanyahu" (Zartman 1997, 209). Although a Palestinian protogovernment, the Palestinian Authority (PA), was established, the new Israeli government delayed the implementation of other—notably territorial—parts of the agreement. Popular frustration rose among the Palestinians, encouraged by the Muslim Salvation Movement (Hamas) riding on the frustration to further its anti-Oslo campaign. As a result, PA president Yasir Arafat, a politician more accomplished as a survivor than as a deliverer, found himself riding a tiger, forced by his desire to follow public opinion to condone and eventually participate (through his al-Aqsa Brigades) in the mounting violence.

The Israeli government's opening of a tunnel along the Western Wall of the Temple Mount in September 1996 led to popular riots in the West Bank, a vigorous Israeli Army (IDF) response, and many Palestinian deaths. The vicious circle continued over the following years: Israeli blockage, Palestinian frustration and reaction, Israeli takeover of West Bank lands through settlements, Hamas attacks, IDF exactions, and so on. The visit of Ariel Sharon to the Temple Mount in September 2000 triggered the second Intifada, which in turn was met by heavily increased Israeli violence against civilian populations and the reoccupation of Palestinian lands, both by the IDF and by continued settlements.

The striking element in this mutually reactive cycle was the refusal and inability of Israel to practice the basic strategy for dealing with spoilers, that is, to encourage the moderates and separate them from the extremists (Stedman 1997). Instead, the Israeli strategy was to provoke the Hamas extremists with military measures and diplomatic obstacles, weaken the PA moderates with repression, provide no incentives to the moderates for cooperation, and then respond with state terrorism against civilians, creating indissoluble solidarity between the extremists and the wider population. As the Israeli mother of a suicide bomber victim cried to the prime minister, "Israel raises terrorists. My daughter's death is the direct consequence of the humiliation inflicted on the Palestinians. . . . We invented these kamikazes. They sacrifice themselves because we have made their lives without value in their own eyes" (Enderlin 2002, 85). Israel correctly came to view Arafat no longer as a moderate but as one of the extremists because they (incorrectly) treated him as such.

State violence after Oslo was a policy of successive Israeli governments, led by the original opponents of the peace agreements, with variations from government to government, designed directly—under Netanyahu and Sharon—and indirectly—under all governments' settlement and repression policies—to undermine the agreements Israel had signed. Militia violence by Hamas, Hizb Allah, al-Aqsa Brigades, and others was spoiler violence by extremists that gradually won over moderates in the PA and the population, with the cooperation of the Israeli extremists in and out of power.

CONGO-BRAZZAVILLE

Among other cases involving militias, Congo-Brazzaville participated in Africa's second wave of democracy in the early 1990s by holding a Sovereign National Conference and opening the former single-party political processes to multiparty elections (Zartman and Vogeli 2000). The new parties immediately reached into their surest sources of support and became tribal organizations, none of them capable of winning a majority but all open to the unstable game of continually seeking the best coalition possible. Unaccustomed to political competition, the party leaders also built militias out of fellow ethnic brothers and plentiful mercenaries to be found among unemployed youth and refugees from neighboring Congo-Kinshasa and beyond. When the leaders finally signed a peace agreement in Libreville in August 1993, they were unable to bring their militias into compliance; "follower-led" violence continued amidst incredible horror, until finally exhaustion broke the "kill or be killed" logic of the ethnic security dilemma six months later (Posen 1993).

Despite provisions in the Libreville Accord, the militias were not disbanded, and when the new presidential campaign began in 1997, they were all poised for action. A campaign incident in May and government charges of a planned coup by former dictator Denis Sassou Nguesso led to the banning of all militias and then to an all-out civil war when enforcement of the ban was attempted. The previously elected president, Pascal Lissouba, was overthrown by the Cobras of Sassou in October; however, the Zulus of Lissouba and the Ninjas of former premier Bernard Kolelas took to the bush to continue the war until finally enticed into a negotiated surrender and amnesty in December 1999, again largely because of exhaustion.

In the first period, negotiations in Libreville were accompanied by a ceasefire in Brazzaville, more or less observed while the leaders talked with the help of international mediation. But wounds were too fresh and tempers too high for the ceasefire and ensuing agreement to hold. Both government and rebel militias renewed their combat, dragging their political leaders along to protect and avenge their followers. It took neutral parliamentarians to arrange another ceasefire and a national peacekeeping force to restore the original peace agreement. But the major leaders kept their militias as insurance, and the insurance forces started the fire in the second period. If government as well as rebel militias imposed their violence after the peace agreement in the first period, they operated as arms of both the government and rebels to reopen the civil war in the second.

Haiti

Haiti also opened its political system to democracy in 1991 after the overthrow of the Duvalier regimes, but its newly elected president, Jean-Bertrand Aristide, was overthrown in turn by his military six months later. During the following two years, international negotiations continued while militias supporting the government carried out a reign of terror against any potential opposition. In July 1993 the junta led by Raoul Cedras finally signed an agreement at Governor's Island, which he proceeded to dismantle on his return, while the "attachés" (militias) continued their exactions against the population. When peacekeeping forces were preparing to disembark from Harlan County in October, militias again threatened civil war if they landed, which they did not. Even when an amnestied withdrawal from power was negotiated with Cedras and U.S. troops landed to monitor the return of Aristide in September 1994, the militias continued to operate, eventually giving way over the rest of the decade to exactions by the new government's militias.

Militias in Haiti continued their operations after the signature of the Governor's Island Agreement by the government they supported, a clear indication along with other actions of the junta's intention not to honor its agreement. It may be argued that the junta was the creature of the militias, or at least that they operated on their own agenda parallel to that of the juntas. But even the latter interpretation is recognition that the government junta and militias alike had no intention of implementing an agreement that they signed primarily to have the sanctions lifted.

Guatemala

Guatemala is a case in which excessive military influence and violence has been a long-lasting and widespread problem—throughout the peace negotiations and after the signing of the final peace accords between the government and the Guatemalan National Revolutionary Unity (URNG) in December 1996. Brokered with support from the United Nations and "Friends," the agreement outlined reform in a vast number of areas, including indigenous rights, human rights, and socioeconomic and military issues.

During the armed conflict, the military obtained powers and privileges that went well beyond the war against the guerrilla movement (Schirmer 1998; de Leon 1998). When negotiations to end the armed conflict were underway in early 1990, the hard-line military saw the peace process as a threat to their power and resorted to violence to undermine moves toward a negotiated settlement. It was commonly believed that the military was involved in a substantial part of the violence during the transition to peace, for instance, in the killing of prominent politician Jorge Carpio in 1993 and the head of the Constitutional Court in 1994. At the same time, a more moderate strand within the military had realized the necessity of the Guatemalan state, and the military in particular, to restore its legitimacy and international reputation, which had been tarnished because of the military's gross human rights crimes. In the end, therefore, the military came to accept a negotiated settlement of the conflict.

Although significant changes have been made within the Guatemalan military and police, disproportionate military influence within the state continues to be a problem in the post-accord period. This is demonstrated by the Arzú government's 2001 defense budget, which almost reversed the reductions stipulated in the peace accord (Sieder et al. 2002, 13). Since 1996 the military has been implicated in violence on several occasions. One incident that stands out both in its gruesomeness and its effect on the implementation of the peace accords is the killing of Catholic bishop Juan Gerardi, beaten to death with a concrete block in April 1997, just two days after he had presented a report documenting the military's extensive human rights abuses during the war. At the time, no one could prove a political motive, but the timing and the circumstances surrounding the killing indicated military involvement in an attempt to undermine the peace process.

The years after the signing of the peace accords have seen a sharp upsurge in violent attacks and threats against activists and professionals within the human rights community, the judicial system, academia, and journalism. While much of the violence in Guatemala is of a criminal nature, there is widespread agreement locally and internationally that the assaults are linked to the activities of clandestine groups that are working to protect powerful individuals. These appear to have ties both to the state and the military and to organized crime (Peacock and Beltrán 2003).[5] Continued violence with links to the security apparatus has guaranteed continued polarization within Guatemalan society, in particular between the Catholic Church and the human rights community on the one hand, and the government and the military on the other hand. This has made reconciliation between the various sectors within Guatemalan society virtually impossible.

Guatemala illustrates the problem of dealing with spoiler violence when there are no strong civil powers to counteract the military. The difficulties in implementing the peace accords in Guatemala stem largely from the fact that neither of the parties that negotiated the final agreement—the government and the URNG—had any great amount of public support (Stanley and Holiday 2002, 423). Civil society has not been able to fill the power vacuum created by the weakness of Guatemala's political actors. This has resulted in continued military influence that undermines the rule of law in the post-accord society. While a return to armed conflict at this stage seems unlikely, disillusionment with the peace process is widespread. The inability of the government to respond effectively to crime has resulted in a general desire for law and order and paved the way for a return of retired hard-line General Rios Montt to the political scene. Thus, while the armed conflict has ended, Guatemala remains an exceptionally violent society.

SOUTH AFRICA

In South Africa state complicity in the war between Inkatha and the African National Congress (ANC) and in violence by extreme right-wing militias remained a source of controversy throughout the transition leading up to the country's first democratic elections in 1994. Violence was used by political opponents of the process and the military to hinder its progression, but it was also used by the main parties of the negotiations to demonstrate their commitment to the cause and as an outlet for frustration among their own followers (Zartman 1995).

Evidence now exists that indicates that high-ranking officers in the military supported the financing, training, and arming of the Zulu-dominated Inkatha Freedom Party (IFP) as a "third force" in the struggle against the ANC during the first years of negotiations. At a later stage, the government took actions to end those activities, but the "third force" still received support from individuals within the state apparatus that feared the demise of apartheid.[6]

There were also fears that right-wing groups with military connections would work to disrupt the peace talks. These fears were bolstered by incidents such as the assassination of ANC leader Chris Hani by a right-wing extremists, the attempt by armed Afrikaners to take control of the black homeland of Bophuthatswana in March 1994, and a bomb campaign in connection to the 1994 elections.

Indeed, violence by the white right-wing and the conflict between Inkatha and ANC threatened to end the entire process on recurring occasions. Often-cited incidents are the Boipatong massacre and the assassination of Hani. However, the deterioration of the already strained economy and fears of a new civil war eventually made both the ANC and the National Party government more determined in their efforts to pursue peace and marginalize the extrem-ists. For instance, after deliberately discontinuing support of the Afrikaner extremists and to the IFP, most of the right-wing parties on both sides were brought into the peace process in the final stage (see, for example, Ohlson 1998, 170; Sisk 1995).

After the formal end of apartheid in 1994, state power changed as the ANC became the largest party and a government of national unity was formed. However, violence has continued to be a prevalent feature of the South African society. While much of the violence in the post-accord period has been local and criminal in character, there are some elements of state collusion. For instance, the conflict between ANC and IFP supporters, which was particularly violent in the province of KwaZulu-Natal, kept on at a high level after the 1994 elections and did not start to decline until after the local elections in 1996. Paramilitary structures of both the ANC and IFP remained active, and there are strong indi-cations that the apartheid-era third-force elements continued to operate after 1994 for reasons related to local power struggles and economic profits, both part of the apartheid legacy (Taylor 2002). The inability of the South African govern-ment to deal with violence in an effective manner has undermined the legitima-cy of the government and inhibited peace-building efforts.[7]

NORTHERN IRELAND

The Northern Ireland case illustrates that even when state collusion in violence is limited to individual soldiers and policemen, it might be an upsetting factor in a peace process. Violence by the loyalist paramilitaries has been commonplace throughout the conflict. While these groups may not be militias in the sense the term has been used in the other cases, they see themselves as fighting a cause on behalf of and for the protection of Northern Ireland; however, they have acted with only tacit support from some unionists and without the support of the British government. Rather than doing a job that the state cannot do, they have performed activities that the state simply will not do.

Alleged state collusion in loyalist violence, however, has been a matter of con-troversy and has led to several investigations in recent years. Individual members of the security forces sympathetic to the belief that the state was not doing its utmost to combat republican terrorism has lent support to the loyalist groups. Some of these have been arrested and are facing charges of involvement in loyalist terrorism. The demand for security-sector reform by the republicans—involving the dismantling of British security installations, the withdrawal of troops, and the reform of police—has been a particularly sensitive issue in the post-accord period and has been fuelled by alleged state collusion in violence. This has been accompanied by demands from the unionist side that the Irish Republican Army (IRA) decommission their arms. The threat of downsizing and dismantling the security apparatus has made many security personnel disillusioned with the peace process (Darby and Mac Ginty 2002).

The Northern Ireland negotiations were exposed to violence from both the mainstream republican and the loyalist paramilitary organizations that agreed to a ceasefire in 1994. However, the parties were largely successful in dealing with spoiler violence during the negotiations leading up to the peace agreement in 1998. Deliberate efforts were made to regulate the use of violence through the so-called Mitchell principles. In this way, mainstream paramilitary groupings, both republican and loyalist, were brought into the political process and became legitimate political actors, leaving little space for extremist groups.

Splits on both sides, however, have resulted in the establishment of new groups opposed to the peace process. Loyalist splinter groups, such as the Loyalist Volunteer Force (LVF), emerged during the negotiation process. These groups, working to derail the peace process, have targeted the Catholic community as well as members of their own side. A killing that has received considerable attention is the murder of Catholic human rights solicitor Rosemary Nelson in March 1999. Loyalist and republican paramilitary groups have been involved in punishment beatings and killings of so-called antisocial elements. In their view, they are upholding law and order in the absence of state action, thus performing some quasi-state functions. In this way, violence with sectarian, political, and criminal intents has continued and seriously put in question the ceasefire of the paramilitaries and the benefits of the peace accord. This has added to the public's general discontent with the peace process, which has resulted in the more extreme political parties gaining support at the expense of the moderate parties. The instability of the peace process has manifested itself in the suspension of the Northern Ireland assembly on recurring occasions.

CONCLUSIONS

Conventionally, studies of peace processes have tended to focus on the rebel groups doing the fighting and returning to war. Violence perpetrated or facilitated by the state or its allies also deserves attention (Stedman 2003). When the state itself, its cohorts, or elements in favor of the state become a source of crime and violence in the post-accord period, a result is lack of legitimacy in the agent who usually not only is responsible for most of the implementation of the peace agreement but also for upholding law and order.

Because of the nature of the cases cited, the conclusions of this investigation are merely supported hypotheses rather than firm findings. It will remain to more comprehensive studies to establish more reliable results. The value of the tentative conclusions presented here is their confirmation of single or contradictory trends in different circumstances, opening up choices for policy and possibilities for research into the most important practical and analytical questions: which, when, why? When two outcomes of the same situation or event are not only logically but also empirically possible, the next step in research is to determine the different conditions that make each likely.

The fear of peace versus fear of war dichotomy provides some insights into the varying effects of state violence and spoiler management. In South Africa, Congo-Brazzaville, Ulster, and Oslo (Israel-Palestine), peace negotiations were driven forward by the fear of continued armed conflict. In the post-Oslo period in Israel-Palestine, the post-Washington period in Angola, and the post-Libreville period in Congo-Brazzaville, failure to deal effectively with spoiler violence completely ruined any trust built between the parties, and fear of peace resurged. But how can the fears of peace be alleviated so as to both prevent spoilers from emerging and mitigate the effects of spoiler violence? How can the opportunities provided by violence be seen and seized by the parties themselves and by concerned third parties? External factors proved to be important in bringing about a change in the Guatemalan military, but how can these changes carry over to the post-agreement period?

This study has shown that positive as well as negative uses of violence can occur during negotiations. As seen in South Africa, Angola, and Haiti, parties sincerely negotiating—that is, opting for the settlement track over the conflict track in their decision making—can at the same time make tactical use of violence to enhance their negotiating position. In such cases, it is wrong for the other party—assuming that it too has shifted from the conflict to the settlement track—to use the violence as an excuse to break off negotiations, thus allying itself with spoilers on the opponents' side. Indeed, even when the other party is using violence during negotiations to give its opponent an excuse to break off talks and bear the blame for doing so, the targeted party should not fall for it if it is sincerely committed to seeking a peaceful settlement. However, while a party directly taking part in negotiations may use violence as a bargaining tool or insurance policy, this kind of violence is liable to be taken as a confirmation that the violence maker is not to be trusted. Mediators, therefore, play an important role in building confidence by verifying commitment to the process, by identifying the agent, and by interpreting the intent behind possible violations (Stedman and Rothchild 1996, 29).

In the post-agreement cases of state violence the motives are less ambiguous. The record in Haiti, Israel, and Congo-Brazzaville shows that states using violence against the other party in the settlement are spoilers, taking advantage of the settlement to break the stalemate and achieve the defeat that could not be obtained before the settlement. Such state action is violence put to negative use in post-agreement situations, that is, used to undermine an agreement that the government has signed unwillingly or without conviction. The undermining attempt may not even be total; the state may simply be trying to regain advantages it lost in the agreement or continue some leftover business that it could not finish before the settlement was signed. In Guatemala elements associated with the state are using violence to hold on to privileges acquired during the armed conflict, such as impunity for criminal offenses. Clearly, the effect is subversive to settlement.

However, the settlement also creates a new context that makes some state involvement in violence in a post-accord phase more ambiguous. An aspect closely related to the seriousness of the threat of post-agreement spoiler violence is the capacity and support of the actor committing the violence and not just the state spoilers' objectives and intent (Stedman 2003). One question is whether the perpetrator is acting autonomously or has significant support, either from a state in the peace process or from the public in general. For instance, the Afrikaner right wing could not hinder the transition or prevent the implementation of the peace accords in South Africa because it did not enjoy enough support within the security forces, while Hamas and the IDF can stop the process because of support from the official parties (protostate and state) and their publics. Whereas it was quite clear that hardliners connected to the Guatemalan military attempted to prevent negotiations and militias in South Africa attempted to influence negotiations before the final accords were signed, today the political purposes of violence there are not that obvious. Much evidence points to the fact that the violence makers in Guatemala and South Africa today are driven by criminal motivations, but the evidence is less clear as to what extent the criminal elements are conducting state—or state-condoned—violence (Call and Stanley 2002). Thus, an important question to consider is under what conditions criminal violence also can be—or should be allowed to be—a threat to peace implementation. Criminal violence should be treated as criminal and not be given a political intent.

But such violence can have other consequences for the state itself in the post-settlement context. Power struggles within the state will be exacerbated during the negotiations and after an accord is signed. As shown in cases such as Northern Ireland, these struggles can manifest themselves in formerly prostate actors targeting the state itself if they believe the state has compromised too much. Violence by the rebels or criminal violence can increase the population's disillusionment with the peace process; playing on these fears, hardliners can come to power or gain prominent positions, as in Israel, Guatemala, and Northern Ireland, in part because they argue that they will be tough—that is, violent—on violence.

One common theme in these cases is the danger of disillusionment within the post-accord society. Violence continues to be a prevalent element of society in South Africa, Israel, Palestine, Congo-Brazzaville, Haiti, Guatemala, and Northern Ireland, hindering reconciliation and peace building. It is obvious that elements of the state and prostate groups are to some extent involved in this violence. While optimism often characterizes the period just after a peace agreement, the post-accord government is confronted with problems similar to those before the war but with the added problems of deep social divisions, a weak economy, and corrupted political institutions. In addition, the state response to crime and political opposition has to change radically. In Northern Ireland and South Africa, proposals for new antiterrorist legislation sparked much discussion since they evoked memories of the armed struggle, in which detention without trial was common practice. The Palestinian Authority was put under pressure to combat terrorism although it lacked either the political or technical means to do so, given the lack of incentives from the other side.

State violence after agreements tends to be subversive to the agreement in intent and effect. But even without spoilers, settlements create a new political and security situation, comprising huge challenges and tasks and weakened authorities and institutions, that creates conditions propitious to violence and to pressures on the state to be involved in it.

NOTES

1. "Spoilers" will be used here to refer to those who disrupt the process as well as the outcome of negotiations, as defined in note 3.

2. The conceptualization of the motives behind violence and the impact of violence on peace making have been advanced in recent research. See in particular research by John Darby (2001) and forthcoming work by Timothy Sisk, "Beyond Bloody Sunday: Violence and Negotiation in Peace Processes." None of these studies, however, have focused specifically on state violence.

3. "Spoilers" have been defined as "leaders and parties who believe that peace emerging from negotiations threaten their power, worldview, and interests, and use violence to undermine attempts to achieve it" (Stedman 1997, 5). An emerging literature on spoilers has sought to critique, modify, and widen the

scope of the concept. See, for instance, the work by John Darby (2001), Thomas Ohlson (1998), Stephen John Stedman (2003), and Marie-Jöelle Zahar (2003).

4. *New York Times*, August 28, 2003, A7.

5. After an agreement was reached in March 2003 to form an international commission to investigate clandestine networks and their ties to state agents, these activities are now about to be investigated. The commission will be called the CICIACS (Commission for the Investigation of Illegal Bodies and Clandestine Security Apparatus) and be composed of three commissioners: one appointed by the Guatemalan government, one by the United Nations, and one by the Organization of American States.

6. Although violence by the so-called third force remains a contested issue, plenty of evidence now exists that describes the involvement of the state and its security forces in violence during the transition. For an overview of the different theories concerning violence during the South African peace process, see, for instance, Du Toit (2001) and Guelke (2000).

7. Since the 1994 elections there have been occasional attacks by right-wing groups discontented with post-apartheid South Africa. However, there is little evidence to indicate that these groups can pose a serious threat to the government. Nonetheless, the continued activity of the white right-wing highlights the underlying racial divisions that continue to dominate South African society (Schönteich 2003).

Marie-Jöelle Zahar

Political Violence in Peace Processes

Voice, Exit, and Loyalty in the Post-Accord Period

The consolidation of peace is a road fraught with dangers, and the emergence of spoilers has been rightfully identified as one of the most serious and frequent threats menacing a nascent and fragile peace in post-conflict societies. In a recent contribution to the debate on contemporary peacemaking, Stephen J. Stedman—who launched the debate on spoilers—identifies them as the number one priority in peace implementation (2003, 106). Stedman defined "spoilers" as actors who believe that peace "threatens their power, worldview, and interests, and use violence to undermine attempts to achieve it" (1997, 5). Many have read into this definition a necessary correspondence between opposition to peace and resorting to violence. This chapter suggests that the correspondence is neither necessary nor theoretically sound. Violence, I contend, is but one of the many strategies available to actors who seek to undermine a peace process as well as to those seeking to join it. As the most extreme manifestation of opposition to peace, the violence perpetrated by militants and ex-militants has been granted primacy in research on the phenomenon of spoiling, contributing in the process to a confla-tion between violence, spoiling, and opposition to peace.

This chapter seeks to answer specific questions: When and for what purpos-es do militants and ex-militants use violence in the aftermath of a peace agree-ment? What kind of barriers can concerned outsiders erect to prevent violence in the post-agreement phase? The chapter thus reframes the spoiler debate by sit-uating it in the broader context of post-conflict violence by nonstate political actors. I propose a framework to this effect, based on the concepts of voice and exit as initially developed by Hirschman (1970). I argue that peace imple-menters, concerned about the sustainability of peace agreements, ought to focus on the interplay between motivation and context. I further identify capability and opportunity as two contextual variables of crucial importance to the deci-sion making of militants and ex-militants considering the use of violence.

SPOILERS IN PEACE PROCESSES: EMPIRICAL AND THEORETICAL PROBLEMS

This chapter seeks to overcome what I believe to be serious limitations of the spoilers debate. To do so, however, requires a quick summary of the broad lines of argument that have until now dominated the discussion. To the question, "Why do peace processes fail?" analysts have identified spoilers as the most pow-erful answer. Indeed, the emergence of spoilers has been blamed for the failure of negotiated settlements, of which Rwanda's genocide stands out as the most egregious. Spoilers are not a mere academic preoccupation. They create serious problems in the stage of peace implementation. The situation in Iraq following the American ouster of Saddam Hussein provides a glaring illustration of the problems caused by spoilers. Not only do spoilers destabilize the security situa-tion, causing more civilian casualties with each violent attack, they can also delay or block international efforts at reconstruction, as the attack on the UN head-quarters in Baghdad and the subsequent pullout of UN workers starkly illustrat-ed. In different circumstances, spoilers can even force troop-contributing nations to pull out of peacekeeping efforts. The death of 231 marines in an attack on their barracks in 1983 in Beirut and the subsequent security deterio-ration prompted then U.S. president Ronald Reagan to order the withdrawal of the marines who were deployed in Lebanon as part of a multinational peacekeep-ing force.

Analysts identify two sorts of spoilers: actors who are located outside the peace process and actors included in the process who subsequently renege on their commitments.[1] Spoiler management means either bringing outsiders into the negotiation process or preventing insiders from developing incentives to renege in the course of implementation. Thus, the sustainability of peace is said to depend in large part on the ability of international custodians to craft and implement efficient strategies for protecting peace and managing spoilers.[2] This focus on international actors as the linchpin of peace has provided a first line of criticism of the spoiler research program.

The current research program on spoilers places excessive weight on the role of third parties in spoiler management. Most analyses of failed peace settlements determine that third parties are critical to the success of peace settlements and the management of spoilers (see Walter 1997). Custodians not only manage spoilers by identifying them and developing strategies to deal with them; they can also act at a broader structural level. Indeed, a variation on the theme has framed spoiling in the context of the security dilemma and singled out demobilization as an especially thorny issue.[3] Even adversaries who truly wish to resolve their conflicts remain wary of disarmament, as weapons are their only means of protection against the unilateral defection of others. Hence, the emergence of spoilers is less an act of malevolence vis-à-vis the peace process and more a function of the rules of the game in an anarchic context. In this framework, outside intervention can serve the purpose of enforcing the terms of the contract.[4] But security dilemmas and commitment problems offer an undifferentiated analysis of civil wars. They also offer undifferentiated solutions. While the involvement of external actors may go a long way toward reassuring former enemies, the strategic situation of actors continues to matter for decision making even with the presence of custodians. This suggests that some peace agreements may be more vulnerable to spoiling than others. It also suggests that it is not international presence per se that is the determining factor. "Scholars do not treat international attention and commitment as a contextual variable, and by defining it as international will make the error of treating it as completely voluntarist" (Stedman 2003, 105–6). Yet, third parties can do too much or too little, and their actions will affect the opportunity structure available to would-be spoilers. In other words, implementers need to be attuned to the context in which they are operating.[5]

The literature has also sought to develop typologies of spoilers. Most notable in this respect is the work of Stephen Stedman, who argued that spoilers vary on two dimensions: their goals (limited or total) and their commitment to the achievement of these goals (high or low). Critics suggested that a central weakness of research on spoilers was its inability to determine spoiler types *ex ante*. The criticism could have been read as a purely academic concern with the predictive power of theories were it not also a logical consequence of the assertion that information and a correct diagnosis of the type of spoiler are crucial for the choice of an appropriate strategy of spoiler management. Yet, as I argued elsewhere, the difficulty lies in the fact that most parties to a civil war both desire peace (as war is costly) and want to get away with as much as they can in the event of an agreement (they have incentives to defect for unilateral gains) (Zahar 2003, 115). In my own work on spoilers, I proposed an alternative way of building spoiler typologies by focusing on the relationship between three factors: intent, or the reasons that may motivate groups or individuals to spoil a peace process; capability, or the resources available to the groups and individuals to this end; and opportunity, or the constraints on spoiling posed by the presence and commitment of foreign interveners (Zahar 2003, 115). I also suggested that intent alone was insufficient to explain spoiling and that it required some level of capability and opportunity to be activated. In other words, the focus ought to be on both sides of the ledger: the motivation of potential spoilers and the context of peace implementation, or what others have also termed "the conflict environment" (Stedman 2003, 108).

In summary, the current research program on spoilers, while novel and promising, has stumbled on two major obstacles. It is currently unable to determine spoiler types with certainty, and it puts too much undifferentiated emphasis on the role of foreign custodians in peace processes. In the rest of this contribution, I argue that a major weakness of research on spoilers—the conflation between two separate phenomena, objection to peace and resorting to violence—may be at the root of both bottlenecks. I therefore propose to recast the debate on spoilers by inserting it in a larger debate on the use of violence in peace processes.

EXIT, VOICE AND LOYALTY: ECONOMIC AND POLITICAL RATIONALES IN PEACE PROCESSES

In his 1970 book *Exit, Voice and Loyalty,* Albert Hirschman proposes a simple but powerful idea: the existence of an inverse relationship between exit and voice. There are, he maintains, two main types of reactions to discontent within organizations to which one belongs: voicing dissatisfaction while remaining a member, or exiting the organization. Exit is a typical economic rationale underlying competition between firms. When one does not like the quality of a product, one changes suppliers. Voice, on the other hand, is the quintessential political instrument (Hirschman 1978). Although both voice and exit are theoretically needed as indicators of an organization's performance, there are ceilings beyond which both can become disruptive. Hirschman thus argues, "Every organization . . . navigates between the Scylla of disintegration-disruption and the Charybdis of deterioration due to lack of feedback."[6] In this constant pull and push, loyalty toward the organization may sway the choices of actors.[7]

Do voice and exit clearly map onto satisfaction and discontent? Would it not be possible for a discontented person to remain within the organization without exiting? While this is clearly a theoretical possibility, I argue that it is highly unlikely in the context of peace implementation. Indeed, as I have argued elsewhere, militants and ex-militants who are dissatisfied with the peace process have a narrow window of opportunity to voice their dissatisfaction. As demobilization proceeds apace and as the dividends of peace deepen, actors are trapped in a "politics of moderation," and the costs of returning to violence increase while the probability of successful derailment of peace decreases (Zahar 2003). For militants and ex-militants whose political influence, personal prestige, economic well-being, and sometimes sheer survival are on the line, the costs of silence (doing nothing) are too high. It is only rational that such actors attempt to either exit the peace process or steer the course of its implementation while they still can.[8]

The voice-exit framework can be usefully extended to the analysis of internal conflicts (and by extension peace processes) because it maps on to the greed-grievance debate that has occupied analysts of civil wars and post-conflict reconstruction in recent times. A basic version of this debate would read as follows. There are two types of actors in civil wars; some follow an economic rationale—war to them is a means to an economic end—and others follow a political rationale—they fight to attain political objectives.[9] Greedy actors are not interested in peace but rather in the pursuit of profit, which is harmed by peaceful environments; therefore, they will always choose exit from peace. In the conflict resolution literature, this exit is labeled spoiling. Actors with grievances want these grievances addressed. In other words, they seek voice and, on this basis, can be brought into peace agreements. In this pared-down version, greedy actors follow economic rationales and will always favor exit over voice. Likewise, actors with grievances follow political rationales and will therefore favor voice over exit.

To be analytically useful, however, the analogy between exit/voice and greed/grievance requires fine tuning. Critics have persuasively argued that greed and grievance are not polar opposites but rather two different types of motivations that can coexist in varying proportion to one another. Moreover, the correspondence between greed and exit is not perfect; nor is that between grievance and voice. Greedy actors have been included in peace processes (though they may not have elected to stay in) when they were lured in by near monopolistic control over the production and allocation of resources. In Sierra Leone, the Revolutionary United Front (RUF) leader Foday Sankoh was offered the post of minister of natural resources. In Mozambique, Renamo was offered a number of material incentives to join the peace process. Voice can therefore be used in an attempt to soothe greedy actors. Further, not all groups acting upon grievances want to be included in peace processes. Hardliners can sometimes refuse to join in any process involving compromise. This, some argue, is the reason why American mediators chose not to deal with the Bosnian Serb leadership in the lead-up to the Dayton Peace Agreement (Holbrooke 1999). A lot has been written about such actors under the label "total spoilers."[10]

In other words, actors with largely political rationales have sometimes chosen exit, while actors with predominantly economic rationales have not always rejected voice. These observations lead me to make two analytical distinctions: first, that violence can theoretically be used in an attempt to express voice as well as to signify exit; second, that it is factually incorrect to conflate spoiling with violence and that such conflation creates analytical problems not only for the diagnosis but also for the management of violence after the signing of peace agreements.

INSIDERS AND OUTSIDERS: CLARIFYING THE LINK BETWEEN SPOILING AND VIOLENCE

I have suggested elsewhere that an important notion in assessing intent to spoil revolves around the distinction between inside and outside spoilers (Zahar 2003, 118–19). I asserted the existence of analytically important differences between militants excluded from peace agreements who elect to use violence and militants included in an agreement whose spoiling expresses a rejection of its terms. I have since come to believe that a more useful distinction must take into account not only the position of actors vis-à-vis a given peace agreement but also the variety of motives underlying their resort to violence. This further differentiation is necessary to understand the uses to which violence is being put; in other words, it allows us to distinguish analytically between violence that seeks to secure voice and violence that expresses exit.

As analytical categories to understand spoiling, the labels "insider" and "outsider" are useful only up to a point. There is no theoretical a priori reason why insiders would necessarily be favorable to peace and outsiders opposed to it. As Stedman forcefully argues, one cannot eliminate the possibility of strategic deception and "blithely [assume] that all parties that sign peace agreements do so in good faith, or are equally trustworthy" (Stedman 2003, 107). Yet, one cannot assume strategic deception a priori. If insiders and outsiders can equally be favorable or opposed to a specific peace agreement, this suggests that these groups have a number of strategic options theoretically available to them (see table 3.1).

TABLE 3.1: STRATEGIC OPTIONS THEORETICALLY AVAILABLE TO ACTORS

	FAVORABLE TO PEACE	NOT FAVORABLE TO PEACE
INSIDER	Voice (Expressed as participation)	Exit (Expressed as spoiling)
OUTSIDER	Voice (Expressed as violence)	Exit (Expressed as spoiling or disengagement)

Insiders can sometimes enter into peace agreements for strategic considerations—such as securing a lull in the fighting to regroup or buying time while waiting for foreign financial and/or military support. Such insiders, when they use violence, are clearly trying to spoil the peace process. Other actors enter into peace agreements with the full intention of living up to their commitments. In the course of peace implementation, however, they face a security dilemma when their opponents (or the third party implementer of the agreement) attempt to use the peace to eliminate them. Such actors, when they elect to use violence, seek to express their disagreement with the direction taken by the polity.

Outsiders can also see peace as a threat for a number of reasons. For some, peace threatens the logic and underlying fabric that justifies and maintains group cohesion. Such is the case, I argue, of movements like Hamas. Such is also the case of movements motivated by greed and for whom the war is just another instrument to secure profit. But in those instances where groups are sidelined for strategic reasons—either because of their relative insignificance in the eyes of foreign mediators or because someone else opposes their presence at the negotiating table—the decision to use violence is often a means to secure voice and inclusion.

Of note in the preceding discussion is the fact that insiders and outsiders who seek voice in relation to a given peace settlement will usually express this in diametrically opposed ways. For insiders, voice translates into participation, while outsiders may use violence to indicate their yearning for inclusion. Likewise, parties favorable or opposed to a given peace settlement can use violence to differing ends. Parties favorable to the settlement may use the violence to express their discontent with failures in implementation. Parties opposed to the settlement may use the violence to overturn the tables on peace. Saying that the parties resorted to violence tells us little, in this instance, about their position vis-à-vis the peace process. I believe this to be the crucial distinction between the violence currently exerted in the West Bank and Gaza by the Islamic fundamentalist group Hamas (opposed to peace with Israel on principle) and some factions within Fatah, the main Palestinian organization within the Palestinian

Liberation Organization (PLO) (disenchanted with the implementation of the Oslo Accords).

CAPABILITY AND OPPORTUNITY: CONFLICT ENVIRONMENTS AND ACTOR STRATEGIES

Whether they want to use violence to exit the agreement or to voice their disagreement with its implementation, not all groups who want or can use violence following a peace process choose to do so. There are countless examples of unsuccessful demobilization and disarmament programs that have not resulted in a return to fighting (see Gamba 2003). Of these, Northern Ireland and Lebanon provide two excellent illustrations. There are also peace settlements that do not involve disarmament (the Yemen Arab Republic, the operation in Haiti) and others that involve weapons buildups (the Dayton Accords in Bosnia and Herzegovina) (Spear 2002, 141). Nor do all the groups who disagree with the shape of post-conflict environments choose to express their dissatisfaction in a violent way. Many do choose more peaceful, participatory means, as was the case with many Christian political parties in postwar Lebanon. Likewise, while third-party implementers can definitely erect barriers to the use of violence, there are enough instances of peace agreements where the threat of third parties was either unnecessary (South Africa) or insufficient (Angola) to suggest that the presence of third parties is insufficient by itself to explain the absence of violence. While it would be analytically easier to draw a direct causal link between intent and/or capability and the use of violent strategies, the world works in more complex ways.

In making decisions about the potential use of violence, militants and ex-militants assess the costs and benefits of each course of action. Though information is at best partial and incomplete and the rationality of such a cost-benefit calculus is naturally bounded,[11] there are standard categories of costs and benefits that these actors consider (see Zahar 2003, 119–21). For insiders, the use of violence raises the specter of military costs related to the level of demobilization and disarmament already achieved and audience costs—both domestic and international—as well as the loss of whatever peace dividends had accrued to these actors from their participation in the peace agreement. For outsiders, however, violence is only costly militarily. In other words, ceteris paribus, the use of violence by insiders is expected to be more costly than the use of violence by outsiders.

As for the benefits associated with a return to violence, these depend in large part on whether this violence is used to gain voice or signify exit. Violence may be used to gain access to state resources and to secure a voice in the conduct of state affairs. In post-conflict elections, hardliners have often used the threat of a return to fighting in order to secure gains at the ballot box. Indeed, a rational choice analysis suggests that voter uncertainty about the threshold at which hardliners may return to violence explains in great part the consecutive electoral victories of such groups in places like Bosnia.[12] Additional benefits from violence include, among others, a return to the war economy and the disruption of a settlement unfavorable to the party that decides to spoil (the use of the term "spoiling" is justifiable here because the ultimate purpose of the violence is indeed the disruption of the peace process).

The costs and benefits of a return to fighting can be constrained by contextual factors. Such factors have often been discussed piecemeal. This chapter brings them together in an analytical framework, the purpose of which is to develop better predictive tools to recognize situations likely to turn violent and to develop effective tools of violence management. These factors can be grouped under two headings: capability—or the resources available to the groups and individuals to this end, and opportunity—or the constraints on violence posed by the presence and commitment of foreign interveners and by the commitment of other actors to the peace process.

Capability

The first question that actors considering the use of violence need to answer is whether they can sustain a return to fighting. Even though the aim of the violence may not be to disrupt the peace process, there is no guarantee that such disruption will not occur and that the use of violence by one party may not start a downward spiral triggering a return to war. The answer will of course depend on a host of variables, which may differ from one case to the other.[13] As I have argued elsewhere, a larger view of capability includes organizational coherence, leadership, and an ability to mobilize supporters (Zahar 2000). However, two broad categories of factors, often identified as part of a conflict environment that gives rise to spoilers (but that are in fact interested in the phenomenon of violence) deserve further elaboration. Actors considering a return to violence in the aftermath of a peace agreement need a minimal amount of military resources to disturb the peace. The availability of such resources will affect the capacity to use violence whatever the group's baseline in terms of organizational coherence, leadership, or ability to mobilize supporters. In other words, I contend that access to such resources can give the advantage to an otherwise small group over a larger, more organized one. In a post-agreement environment, these resources can still be obtained where actors have access to one of the following assets: (1)

valuable tradable commodities and a regional underground network to produce, ship, and trade these commodities; or (2) foreign patrons with a willingness to provide the groups with military resources.

The absence of readily available weapons to the various factions is paramount to keeping a fragile and nascent peace. "The ending of a civil war hinges on the willingness of competing armies to relinquish self-help solutions to their insecurity, to demobilize their soldiers, and in most circumstances, to create a new, integrated army" (Stedman 2003, 109). Thus, not only disarmament but also genuine demobilization—dismantling the command and control structures of armed groups to make a return to organized violence less likely—is necessary to consolidate the peace (Spear 2002, 141–82).

Where actors have access to regionally based war economies, they can use such financial resources to buy weapons while skirting demobilization and disarmament programs. The regional dimension of war economies has until recently been downplayed in analyses of peace implementation. In an important addition to the literature, Michael Pugh and Neil Cooper (2004) document the existence of regional dynamics that underpin the political economy of conflict; they further argue that the neglect of such dynamics has detrimental effects on our understanding of conflict dynamics and/or the ability to design workable solutions for transition to peace. The existence of regional economic linkages in the form of trade routes, open markets, trading partnerships, and the like often predates the conflict, and even when used for activities that belong to the grey economy, they tend to possess functional aspects. When the war erupts, warlords either seek to control or simply utilize those linkages to finance their military activities.[14] After the war, foreign interveners—the custodians of peace in Stedman's terminology— often fail to grasp the historical and functional dimensions of these linkages, and, consequently, their plans for economic reconstruction do not take these into consideration. As a result, political considerations sometimes trump economic realities. The effort to rebuild the Bosnian economy without tying it to Serbia or Croatia because of the role these two states played during the war illustrates this dynamic inasmuch as it ignored the fact that Bosnia's historical markets were located in Serbia and Croatia. This does not take into account the vital economic connection and the complementarity of these economies.[15] When peace implementation disregards or fails to notice the existence of regional economic linkages and of a regional infrastructure for economic exchanges, the post-agreement experience of many countries—including Sierra Leone, Afghanistan, and Bosnia, to name only a few—shows that these regional complexes survive and provide actors with the means to finance a return to violence.

Where actors have a limited financial base but can count on the support of outside patrons for weapons, disarmament and demobilization are also likely to

TABLE 3.2: CAPABILITY AND TYPES OF CONFLICT ENVIRONMENTS

	REGIONAL WAR ECONOMY	NO REGIONAL WAR ECONOMY
OUTSIDE PATRONS	Extremely volatile conflict environment	Volatile conflict environment
NO OUTSIDE PATRONS	Volatile conflict environment	Stable conflict environment

fail. External forces with a stake in the outcome of a civil conflict can become complicating factors at the negotiating table. "Sometimes such a regional power . . . may see its interests best served by the prolonging of a stalemate until the situation forces a settlement it can accept, rather than commit itself wholeheartedly to the course of conflict resolution" (De Silva and Samarasinghe 1993, 14). Regional actors have often attempted to dictate hard or soft stances to their clients out of self-interest.[16] One need only remind oneself of the relations between Bosnian Serbs and Belgrade, or of the ties between the Lebanese forces and Israel, to make the point. The interests and calculations of outside patrons need not necessarily coincide with the best interests of the war-torn country or the designs of international mediators and peace implementers. The regional ambitions or long-term political goals of external actors, when not achieved in the course of the specific peace settlement, provide these actors with incentives to continue to interfere in the post-agreement politics of the country. When the incentives of outside patrons and the needs of internal actors coincide, the patrons can step in and provide those actors with the military and financial resources necessary to resume the violence.

In brief, I have argued that two factors—the existence of a regional economic complex and the presence of foreign patrons—combine to create particularly unstable conflict environments (see table 3.2). Both make it exceptionally arduous to achieve what Stedman (2003) and Spear (2002) identify as "the *single* most important sub-goal of peace implementation" (Stedman 2003, 109), the demobilization of soldiers.

A correct assessment of capability—in other words, an accurate evaluation of the conflict environment—is particularly important for the custodians of peace as they try to manage the implementation of a given agreement. Indeed, it is the local actors' capability to resort to violence that best indicates the type and extent of foreign intervention necessary to oversee peace implementation. And I have suggested that this capability is partly a function of two factors: war economies and outside patrons. Where regional war economies and outside patrons increase the potential that actors will find resources necessary to rekindle the violence, foreigners will need more muscle, political will, and financial resources to see to it that peace is maintained. It bears repeating that this violence may not necessarily be directed at the peace process but that it will often have repercussions on the extent and success of peace implementation efforts. A good case in point is the situation in Afghanistan, where tribal violence between warlords has little to do with the Bonn peace process. Yet this violence, which is often about control over resources and smuggling routes, as well as a number of regional or local rivalries, is in part responsible for the inability of the International Security Assistance Force (ISAF) to extend its authority outside of Kabul and its suburbs. This begs the question as to whether the peace process would crumble if the ISAF were pulled out of Afghanistan. Such an analysis would further suggest that the conflict environment of the Great Lakes is probably more challenging than that in the Middle East. Both the number of regional actors involved in the conflict in the Democratic Republic of the Congo (DRC) and the regional economic complex work against isolating the conflict in the DRC from its broader environment. On this score the Middle East situation is more promising in view of the separate peace treaties signed between Israel and a number of its Arab neighbors (Jordan and Egypt), as well as the very low level of economic integration in the Arab world in general and between Arab economies and the economic infrastructure of Gaza and the West Bank in particular.

OPPORTUNITY

If capability refers to the resources available to actors considering the use of violence, opportunity refers to the barriers that can prevent violence or make it a costly option. These barriers can be of two kinds. The first and most analyzed remains the commitment of foreign actors to oversee the implementation of the peace process and decisively deal with would-be spoilers. The other, less scrutinized, barrier relates to preventing the use of violence by actors favorable, rather than opposed to, peace: this barrier I call the development of a sense of loyalty to the peace process among all insider actors.

In the immediate aftermath of peace agreements, foreign custodians of peace remain the most effective bulwark against a relapse into violence. In the absence of a functioning central state capable of claiming a monopoly on the use of legitimate violence, it is incumbent upon the custodians to secure the peace (see Stedman 1997). It has been argued convincingly that the most important task at hand is the demobilization of fighters and the dismantling of the command and control structures that could be used to regroup fighters and resume war. The presence of an "impartial" foreign observer is often crucial to oversee such developments. Impartial implementers can strengthen the ability of mechanisms such as ceasefire commissions to prevent a relapse into violence (see Fortna 2004). In the absence of foreign custodians, or when the latter are seen to be too enmeshed in the conflict, as is the case with the Irish and the British in Northern Ireland, the "impartiality" of custodians' assessments of progress on thorny issues can come under scrutiny and contribute to the creation of bottlenecks in the peace process. Another important task is the reintegration of combatants into society. Short of such reintegration, political violence may be stemmed while societal violence will be on the rise.

As argued above, custodians face more or less volatile conflict environments. Implementers need to be attuned to the context in which they are operating. Depending on the challenges emanating from the conflict environment, custodians will need to adopt different types of approaches to the tasks of violence management, including disarmament and demobilization. Where the risks of violence are high, custodians will need not only to commit sufficient troops but also be willing to use them and incur casualties to keep the peace. Indeed, a study of sixteen peace agreements concludes that implementation strategies must be calibrated to the level of difficulty of the case: "In certain limited situations, strategies that derive from traditional peacekeeping (with its underlying emphasis on confidence-building) can be effective. In more challenging situations, however, when predation coexists with fear, confidence-building will prove inadequate, and implementers will need to compel and deter to ensure compliance with a peace agreement" (Stedman 2002, 664).

This conclusion raises the issue of "incentive compatibility," or the fact that the chances of implementation are proportional to the perceived self-interest of critical actors. It also underlines the fact that volatile conflict environments are "difficult implementation environments." While they require more resources, greater involvement, and more coercive strategies, these are often not forthcoming "because no major or regional power perceives peace in a given country to be in its own vital strategic interest" (Stedman 2002, 664). Where major or regional powers have defined peace implementation as a vital strategic interest—as Syria did in Lebanon or NATO in Bosnia—custodian commitment has acted as a barrier against the use of widespread violence by insiders and outsiders alike.

But securing the peace should not be reduced to spoiler management. While this is obviously an important task, custodians of peace can also play a persuasive rather than dissuasive role. For peace to take hold, outsiders need to be brought into the fold or contained, but that should not distract the analyst from the importance and relevance of relations between custodians and insiders. As the experience of Bosnia and Herzegovina has amply demonstrated, threats to peace may not always emanate from the outside; threats may come from the parties involved in the peace process as well. Thus, a second barrier to exit, one less systematically analyzed, is the kind of loyalty that political actors demonstrate toward the peace agreement. This barrier is particularly important to understand the likelihood that insiders will use violence in the post-agreement phase. Indeed, loyalty, whatever its kind, presupposes inclusion, and it cannot, therefore, be used with reference to outsiders or political actors excluded from the negotiation process.

Loyalty is the third and some would say most important construct in Hirschman's exit-voice-loyalty framework. In this framework, loyalty is an exogenous factor that operates to incite dissatisfied customers to exercise voice and exert pressures to reverse the decline in a given organization. However, loyalty is not a necessary prelude to voice (see Barry 1991, 187–221). A person might remain "loyal" to an organization for instrumental reasons (because of the material advantages that the organization provides, in other words, because exit would involve significant material losses) or because he or she perceives the barriers to exit as too great (see Cannings 1992, 262). Though construed as loyalty in the standard literature on exit and voice, these types of attachment are different from commitment to the goals of the organization. A distinction must therefore be made between different kinds of loyalty. Studies of organizational commitment provide an entry point into this distinction. According to these studies, three prime factors enter into organizational commitment (Mowday, Porter, and Steers 1982, 1979). They are (1) a strong belief in and acceptance of the organization's goals and values; (2) a willingness to exert considerable effort on behalf of the organization; and (3) a strong desire to retain membership in the organization. If the first factor represents commitment, the second voice, and the third attachment, it has persuasively been argued that attachment provides a necessary but not sufficient condition for the transformation of loyalty into commitment, with voice representing the organization's contribution to this transformation by making available the necessary channels and the incentives to use them (Cannings 1992, 264–65).

In the same way as the exit-voice framework seemed to parallel the debate on greed and grievance in civil wars, discussions of loyalty parallel debates on the meaning of peace implementation. Implementation can mean three distinct things to different actors and observers: compliance, process, or peace building.[17] Compliance emphasizes a legalistic fulfillment of obligations spelled out in the peace agreement; process underscores the commitment to a continuous negotiation of differences; peace building values the forging of meaningful long-term relationships between former enemies. While all three meanings can definitely coexist in a given post-agreement environment, only the first two correspond to actual strategies adopted by custodians in the framework of peace implementation.[18] The

choice of strategy and the privileging of corresponding loyalty types bear consequences for the sustainability of peace and the likelihood of insider violence.

At the minimum, peace agreements seek to elicit compliance. Indeed, more
often than not such agreements represent pacts between unwilling partners
forced to compromise by their inability to secure a decisive military victory.[19]
Actors involved in these pacts negotiate terms that allow them to maximize gains
in light of the conditions under which they are negotiating. In other words,
peace negotiations occur at a time when both sides, for whatever reason, agree to
accept the military outcome, be it symmetrical or asymmetrical, as the basis for
determining the political payoffs accruing to each (Kecskemeti 1970). Peace
agreements that elicit compliance are particularly vulnerable to insider violence
since attachment to the agreement is a function of expected gains from membership. When expected gains do not become a reality or when gains from a return
to conflict supersede the benefits derived from peace, insiders are likely to
attempt to exit the agreement. A good illustration of this dynamic is provided by
the behavior of UNITA leader Jonas Savimbi's decision to walk out on the
Lusaka Accords because of his failure to secure election to the presidency of the
republic (Lyons 2002, 222). Indeed, even though "Savimbi and UNITA received
more from the Angolan settlement than any of the losing parties in El Salvador,
Mozambique, Nicaragua, and Zimbabwe received in theirs" (Stedman 1996,
370), Savimbi calculated that electoral results—for the presidency and for provincial governorships, of which UNITA was expected to win four out of eighteen—
were "too meager a prize to persuade [him] from trying his luck at winning
power through war" (Ohlson and Stedman 1994, 193).

Even where the military situation forces compromise, incentives are still
required to bring the various factions to the negotiating table. For example, in
the conflict in Bosnia and Herzegovina, the Serb leadership, whose military
power was seriously curtailed by a joint Bosnian-Croat offensive and two weeks
of NATO bombings in August 1995, demanded (and secured) the recognition of
Republika Srpska, the Serb entity within Bosnia and Herzegovina. Mediators
acknowledge that such incentives are not enough to elicit commitment to peace.
Problems of credible commitment plague peace implementation as even actors
interested in peace may not be able to trust their interlocutors to keep their
promises and may therefore prefer to return to fighting. This is the logic behind
the introduction of institutionalized channels for voice, most often secured
through some sort of power-sharing arrangement. While analysts disagree on the
ability of power sharing to secure long-lasting peacekeeping and a move toward
democracy (in other words, the transformation through voice of loyalty into a
commitment to the post-agreement polity), the hope is that at a minimum such
power sharing will prove conducive to a continuous negotiation of differences.

Table 3.3: Opportunity and Likelihood of Insider Violence

	Committed Custodians	Reluctant Custodians
Attachment	No violence	High likelihood of violence
Voice	No violence	Low likelihood of violence
Commitment	No violence	No violence

Under such circumstances, the likelihood of insider violence decreases drastically. Only when the power-sharing formula is tampered with either by a state bent on excluding one of the political actors (Lebanon and the exclusion of Christian opposition forces) or by a custodian seeking to fundamentally reinterpret the bases of power sharing (Bosnia and current attempts by the Office of the High Representative [OHR] to centralize the state) can we then expect insiders to use violence in an attempt to voice their disagreement with the course of peace implementation (see table 3.3).

POLITICAL VIOLENCE IN THE POST-AGREEMENT PHASE: NEW RESEARCH DIRECTIONS

This chapter has sought to reflect on violence in post-accord settings. Using Hirschman's (1970, 1974) voice-exit framework, I argue that a broader, more inclusive understanding of violence must overcome the conflation between violence and spoiling. In the same way that voice and exit are not the two ends of a spectrum but distinct strategies to deal with dissatisfaction, I demonstrate that violence is a strategy used by actors seeking both voice (inclusion in or renegotiation of the peace agreement) and exit (disruption of peace). Other nonviolent strategies available to actors include participation in the political process and disengagement from that process (see table 3.4).[20]

The chapter also develops the concepts of capability and opportunity to provide analysts and practitioners with a rough guide to the conflict environment at hand. Capability, defined as the resources available to militants and ex-militants considering a return to violence, is operationalized as a function of two factors: the presence of a regional economic infrastructure used to generate resources outside of the scope of state authority, and control and the presence of foreign patrons able and willing to provide resources for the resumption of fighting. Opportunity, or the barriers erected to decrease the likelihood of violence, is also a function of two factors: the presence and commitment of custodians, and the

Table 3.4: Voice, Exit, and Actor Strategies in Post-Accord Settings

	Exit	No Exit
Voice	**Voice and exit** Insiders using violence to seek recalibration of the peace agreement. Outsiders using violence to seek inclusion.	**Voice and no-exit** Insiders deciding to play within the rules of the game.
No Voice	**No-voice and exit** Outsiders who spoil.	**No-voice and no-exit** Outsiders and insiders who decide not to use violence but disengage from politics.

type of loyalty generated by the peace agreement among insiders. Together, capability and opportunity define the context in which actors evaluate the costs and benefits of using violence to pursue their objectives and claims. They also provide custodians with standard categories to estimate the likelihood of violence and develop targeted violence-management strategies (see table 3.5).

To paraphrase Stephen Stedman, the meanings ascribed to peace implementation are likely to differ in conflict-ridden societies, but custodians can only ignore progress on any dimension—be it compliance, process, or long-term meaningful relationships—at their own peril (Stedman 2003, 112). Narrow compliance runs the risk of instability and of insider violence. It fails to develop more than an instrumental loyalty to the post-accord setting and makes peace highly dependent on the

Table 3.5: Types of Implementation Environments in Post-Accord Periods

	Capability	Lack of Capability
Opportunity	**Unfavorable implementation environment** Favorable to violence by insiders and outsiders.	**Moderately unfavorable implementation environment** Favorable to violence by insiders.
Lack of Opportunity	**Moderately favorable implementation environment** Favorable to violence by outsiders (spoiling).	**Favorable implementation environment** Not favorable to violence.

continued presence of the custodians. Process without compliance can raise serious questions about the importance of substance and trigger the alienation of insiders concerned that their voice is not being heard. When voice fails to trigger responsiveness, it can prevent the development of deeper commitment to the polity. Instead, it can actually induce violence as actors despair of getting their voice heard otherwise, or, even worse, it can produce disengagement and apathy or the kind of exit that operates on those running the polity "not as an incentive to improve but as a licence to deteriorate" (Barry 1991, 220).

NOTES

1. This "tactical acceptance" thesis is mostly promoted by Donald Horowitz (1985).

2. Custodians have pursued three major strategies to manage spoilers: (1) inducement entails giving the spoiler what he wants (default mode); (2) socialization requires the establishment of a set of norms for acceptable behavior by which to judge the demands and the behavior of parties and involves material and intellectual components eliciting normatively acceptable behavior; and (3) coercion, which relies on the use or threat of punishment to deter or alter unacceptable behavior or reduce the capability of spoilers to disrupt the peace process.

3. According to proponents of this approach, civil wars reproduce the anarchy of the international system where self-help is the only logical course of action. The greatest problem that civil war opponents encounter is how to write an enforcement contract under conditions of extreme risk. Negotiations would succeed in designing peaceful transitions if the participants could be protected during the implementation period. For a discussion of the security dilemma in civil wars, see Posen (1993). On the conditions of peaceful transition, see Walter (1998); a modified version of Walter's argument was subsequently published in International Security 24, no. 1 (1999).

4. See Walter (1997); see also Hampson (1996). This argument is very similar to the standard international relations argument about the role of institutions or regimes in fostering cooperation under anarchy.

5. On the differentiated role of implementers, see particularly the conclusions of Stedman, Rothchild, and Cousens (2002) and Stedman (2001).

6. Hirschman (1974, n.14). Every organization, that is, but the state. Indeed, while exit was and remains common in stateless societies, the consolidation of states has been accompanied by a growing restriction of the conditions for lawful secession.

7. The loyalty concept is the most under-researched aspect of the voice-exit-loyalty model. Some perceive loyalty as an attitude that moderates exit and

voice; others interpret it as a distinct behavioral response to dissatisfaction, on par with exit and voice.

8. For a similar line of reasoning, see Fearon (1998).

9. For a good introduction to the greed and grievance debate, see Berdal and Malone (2000).

10. Total spoilers, or zealots, may provide the one qualification to the usefulness of Hirschman's model in civil war situations. The model does not necessarily provide for actors who wish neither to change the situation from within nor exit and who may instead want it to either collapse or be taken over. Hamas and the splinter republican movements in Northern Ireland provide good examples of this category. However, I bracket this category from the discussion because it does not invalidate the broader argument about the relationship between spoiling and violence.

11. Herbert Simon (1957).

12. For a detailed account of the rationale behind this argument, see Wantchekon (1999).

13. What follows is thus intended as an indicative rather than exhaustive set of variables to consider in making this assessment.

14. This is an important corrective to the literature on war economies, not least of all because it also demonstrates that greed and grievance are not polar opposites but often parallel, if not overlapping, tracks.

15. I am indebted to Susan Woodward for this observation.

16. In the Third World, "the Big Powers' and the superpowers' interventions in civil conflicts have added to their severity and cost and introduced protractedness . . . to what otherwise could have been a less salient set of conflictive interactions" (Azar et al. 1978, 47).

17. For a detailed discussion of the three meanings of peace implementation, see Stedman (2003, 111–12).

18. Because forging long-term meaningful relationships is a long-term objective rather than a short-term strategy, I leave this out of the discussion.

19. Peace settlements are in essence elite pacts established as a transitional strategy toward democratic regimes or outcomes. See Sisk (1996, esp. chap. 5), Hartzell and Rothchild (1997), and Wood (1999).

20. Groups that retreat from political life but do not have the capability to secede would fall under this category. In his article, "Voice, Exit, and the State," Hirschman (1978) discusses two specific types of disengagement: migration and capital flight.

Virginia Gamba

Post-Agreement Demobilization, Disarmament, and Reintegration

Toward a New Approach

The thawing of the Cold War in the late 1980s led the United Nations Security Council and a series of like-minded states acting multilaterally to explore the possibilities for collective management of conflict resolution in regions affected by war or emerging from violent conflict. Beginning in 1989 bigger and more comprehensive and complex multinational peace support operations emerged in many regions: Namibia, Zimbabwe, Mozambique, Liberia, Sierra Leone, Somalia, Cambodia, El Salvador, Nicaragua, Haiti, and Bosnia-Herzegovina were some of the many comprehensive operations launched. Not all were successful in promoting or defending peace, but, taken as a whole, analysis of them assists in determining the challenges that any transition from conflict to peace faces in the contemporary environment.

Control over warring parties, ensuring a peaceful transition to the establishment of a democratically elected government, managing demobilization processes, reviewing defense and security structures to serve the needs of peace time, and establishing law, order, and infrastructures to ensure sustainable development of affected countries are all seen—or should be seen—as part of a continuum. The comprehensive nature of a peace engagement is not disputed today. The early strategies of massively engaging on the ground in order to bring peace and then seeking an early exit without focusing on the consolidation of peace and security in the emerging state are now being replaced by a long-haul process that is unpopular but unavoidable.

This chapter does not seek to provide a historic analysis of what went wrong, where, and why. There is abundant literature to provide this background;[1] rather, it seeks to unpack the Demobilization, Disarmament, and Reintegration (DDR) elements that are fundamental to the comprehensive development of sustainable peace and security in conflict-affected states and their immediate regions. Each one of these elements will then be developed with particular reference to the experience of southern Africa in the last decade.

Finally, the chapter will focus on the corrective mechanisms that the region itself has proposed to ensure sustainability in the provision of peace and security and will analyze what chances the region has, if any, in achieving its goals. By focusing on the case study of southern Africa, I hope to produce a set of recommendations on how to think and implement policies that will empower DDR initiatives to genuinely assist the prevention and management of violence today.

THE MAKING AND CONSOLIDATION OF PEACE: A DDR CONTINUUM

Key objectives of a peace process are to secure peace, ensure demobilization, ensure disarmament, and assist in post-conflict reconstruction and development. If these objectives are not realized, peace cannot be consolidated. Since 1989 almost all cases of multinational peace-making and peace support operations have not fully realized the above-mentioned objectives.

In the study of these peace-making and peace-consolidating initiatives, it is possible to identify two principal problems that, unless addressed early and corrected, will compromise the mission itself and the sustainability of lasting peace. These are (1) problems associated with the establishment and maintenance of a security environment early on, and (2) problems concerned with a lack of coordination of efforts among the regional and international communities, the various groups involved in a peace mission, the peace mission itself, and the postconflict reconstruction effort (UNIDIR 1996–98, 211).

The establishment of security must come first to ensure stability, which requires clear political authority and policy guidelines. The provision of reasonable security to belligerent parties has a direct impact on their willingness to demobilize and disarm. Many failures of the 1980s and 1990s were directly related to this issue, as seen in Angola, Somalia, the former Yugoslavia, Liberia, and Sierra Leone, to name a few.

Similarly, comprehensive coordination ensures unity of command to sustain security during the peacekeeping phase and the cost effectiveness of emergency sustainability of the population in transition. It also influences the ability of sustainable development through the coordinated efforts of the international and regional communities. Lack of coordination impacted almost all the peace support missions since the late 1980s, although more effort in this regard can be seen in relatively successful transitions such as Mozambique, Cambodia, Namibia, Timor, and Haiti.

The truth is that insecurity during the peace process will delay or break the effort, as happened in Angola and Somalia. Likewise, lack of coordination will not only endanger the mission and expose it at the time, but more importantly, it will slow down or scuttle the post-conflict reconstruction phase, where the emphasis lies in the provision of law and order, the creation of infrastructure, the demilitarization of society, and sustainable development.

Ultimately conflict and peace are interrelated. Nowhere is this more evident than in the complex environment of demobilization, disarmament, and reintegration. This happens first because countries impacted by a high level of violence and conflict or outright war have an abundance of weapons. Weapons enter a conflict area as if sucked in. They are not always paid for in the conventional manner because affected countries are more often than not in continents that have been racked by armed conflict for decades. This means that the accumulation of weapons over many years, without a clear policy of disarmament and destruction at the end of each cycle of violence, will be available to any new emerging conflict. The porosity of borders, the weakness of transitional states, the corruption of officials, and the emergence of a more organized network of criminals in and across borders allow for the trafficking of weapons with relative ease. New weapons, illicit weapons from neighboring communities and regions, and the inability to guard and protect legal weapons in possession of the state from negligence or theft make up the majority of arms that find their way to conflict areas. For civilian populations weapons also become a survival tool. These weapons enter civilian hands either through direct issuance by warring parties themselves or through the illicit markets that cash in on the insecurity of peoples living in an environment where they are not assured law and order.

Second, countries in conflict require a large number of military or paramilitary personnel and the ability to replenish this pool of people on a constant basis. Many countries in conflict do not have professional armies, and not all insurgent forces are trained professionally. Conscription may be introduced, and forced recruitment of men, women, and children to feed insurgent movements is also common. High attrition rates of the most untrained, unprofessional, and vulnerable of these people create more and more of the same. Eventually, there will be virtually no one untouched by war. At the same time, it means that the wartime skills of people are very different from those that will be needed in post-conflict reconstruction processes. It also means that people who have survived through the use or the threat of the use of armed violence in one capacity or another will find themselves operating in a changed environment where those skills are not rewarded or replaced. They often turn to crime to survive. For the unemployed, the type of crime associated with post-conflict reconstruction is of two types: common armed banditry and organized crime. For the underemployed (with an insufficient and intermittent salary), the ability to exert power and influence through their standing and their arms and skills will lead to corruption, blackmail, and robbery. In both cases the main victim is the development potential of the country, for without security there is no investment, and without investment no development is possible.

Third, the civilian population and national infrastructures in conflict areas are more often than not the first victims of directed violence. Aside from the normal suffering that civilians always incur in a war, they are also often used as tools of war: the displacement of communities will place an onus on the warring faction that must sustain them; the burning of crops will destroy the sustainability of opponents as well as villagers; the mining of land will ensure tactical demilitarized zones but will become the single most difficult post-conflict reconstruction challenge in rural areas; the issuance of arms to civilian populations will complicate the military operations of an enemy but will create a massive problem with crime and violence in post-conflict reconstruction, and so forth. The collapse of infrastructure follows similar patterns. The destruction of roads, harbors, airstrips, and communication lines will complicate and slow down military operations, but it will also ensure time for warring factions to muster, arm, and train people. The destruction of natural resource extraction and transport infrastructure will deny profits to a warring faction but will harm the ability of the nation to rebuild itself in the future. Perhaps the worst damage to infrastructure that happens in a country affected by conflict is the destruction of governance and oversight procedures and processes of which the legislative and the judicial are the first victims, followed closely by provincial authorities, the media, and civil service in general, and the police and armed forces in particular.

Demobilization, disarmament, and reintegration are therefore a single entity that affects both the chances of peace and the chances of re-creating a secure and safe environment for countries emerging from conflict. In the manner in which these three issues are tackled early on—in the grey period between war and peace—lies the roots of a successful transition or the making of a failed state. It is an issue that needs to be taken seriously, if not for humanitarian reasons then at least for strategic consideration. Here it is important to emphasize that our understanding of what makes a failed state is not conclusive. In this era of shifts and changes and of the deep impact of globalization on the nature of conflict and peace, it is difficult even to define what a failed state is. Nevertheless, it is possible to say that the process leading to a state being categorized as such is necessarily a slow one. Today, as Haass indicates, we also view it in strategic terms:

> A state that no longer has control over its territory, that no longer has credible, unifying institutions, is a threat to its people, its neighbors, and the international community. Diagnosing state failure as both a strategic and a humanitarian problem has implications for how we address it. Strengthening or reforming the institutions of weak states is a priority. And ensuring that new states are born with viable institutions—be it East Timor or Palestine—is a serious responsibility. Those of us who long distinguished between hard and soft areas of security studies need to think again. (Haass 2002, 4)

TAKING STOCK

Between 1990 and 1998 a series of dramatic events in southern Africa led to an internal analysis process in the region that ultimately led to massive policy changes in Africa, the latest of which is the creation of the Africa Union (AU) (Durban, 2002), the consensus on a common policy guideline in the New Partnership for Africa's Development (NEPAD) (Lusaka, 2001), and the establishment of a single AU-NEPAD agenda for peace and security (Addis, February 2003). The internal analysis process and the emerging corrective policies attest to the belief that disarmament and demobilization were never adequately conducted during peace processes in the region.

During the 1990s the region saw the emergence of South Africa as a fully democratic country operating in a changed economic, military, and social environment. It further saw the end of colonialism in southwest Africa with the independence and consolidation of the Namibian republic; the achievement of peace in Mozambique after more than twenty-five years of civil war; the achievement of peace (twice) in Angola and the recurrence of war in both cases; and the changed status of the situation in the Democratic Republic of the Congo (DRC) with the ousting of Mobutu Sese-Seko and the unstable and violent emergence of the Kabila government in Kinshasa in the wake of the Great Lakes crisis, which captured the world's attention with the Rwanda genocide of 1994.

Despite setbacks such as renewed war in Angola, the subregion felt confident that the new-found processes in southern Africa would allow for regional development and the creation of peace structures. Peace and political transition in Zimbabwe, Namibia, and South Africa and the end of two hot wars—that of Mozambique, which turned out to be permanent, and that in Angola, which turned out to be temporary—allowed for regional structures of like-minded states to form and consolidate. This generated the emergence of the Southern African Development Community (SADC) and, associated with it, the emergence of the Southern Africa Regional Police Chiefs Coordinating Committee (SARPCCO) and the Inter-State Defense and Security Committee (of military forces in the region) (ISDSC). These structures, although new and sometimes ad hoc, provided for exchange of information and discussion among member states of the subregion.

Although these structures had emerged with a vision of post-conflict reconstruction and development as their primary focus, they quickly became involved in regional debate on stability and post-conflict reconstruction. The repeated discussions at the forums allowed for the exchange of information on factors that were impinging growth and development at national levels. By 1997 there were three issues that kept emerging in regional debates mobilized by the most affected countries:

- the exponential increase in armed and violent crime (both by individuals and organized criminal groups) in major capitals and the increase in violent conflict resolution dynamics at the community level—often through possession and use of illicit arms
- the perception of displaced, repatriated, badly demobilized ex-combatants and refugee communities in the region as being vehicles for the barter of illegal arms and the increase in criminal activities and political instability
- the continued existence of rebel groups in several areas of southern Africa, as indicated by the tenuous peace in Angola and the military activity surrounding the death of Mobutu Sese-Seko in Zaire

It was clear to all that the increased availability of small arms that had become redundant or surplus to the political needs of combatants tended to find their way to civil society and to criminal organizations. Civil society utilized them either to protect itself or to trade and barter for economic gain, particularly in relation to demobilized but not disarmed soldiers. Invariably, these arms ended up in the hands of criminals or joined the trickle of illegal goods that make up the vast river of illicit trade pipelines in and out of Africa.

Implementing Disarmament

The results of these exchanges led to substantive action on the need for the control of the illicit trade in small arms and light weapons in the region. The analysis of the impact of badly conducted disarmament operations, during peace processes in general and in relation to Mozambique and Angola in particular, served to focus the attention on a massive mopping-up operation that would be regional in character but national in execution. The engine for change on this issue was South Africa.

South Africa, with reduced deterrence capacity due to transitional reintegration and restructuring of its law enforcement capacity and with an increased free flow of people from its immediate subregion, bore the brunt of the consequences of peace without disarmament in Mozambique. After 1993, following peace in Mozambique, small arms collected and not destroyed commenced to escape state control through corruption or the operations of increasingly sophisticated organized crime networks mobilizing arms in and out of Africa to fuel conflict and crime in the region and elsewhere. Furthermore, there had not been a systematic collection of arms in Mozambique, so that only a minor percentage were collected and the rest escaped control by passing into the hands of civilians and demobilized soldiers or remaining in caches underground. South Africa then became the prime end destination and transit point of illicit small arms in the region.

South Africa was not the only country affected. Armed crime not only increased in Durban, Johannesburg, and Cape Town but also in the city of Maputo in Mozambique and the city of Mbabane in Swaziland. Rural areas straddling the three neighbors also became affected with an increase in armed cattle rustling and bandit activity. Weapons starting circulating north to Malawi and Zimbabwe, to eventually find their way to the emerging military conflict in the Great Lakes region. Similarly, illicit weapons moving through Zimbabwe and South Africa found their way to Namibia, Zambia, and southern Angola, destabilizing the potential for peace in Angola.

It was at the 1998 annual general meeting of the police chiefs of southern Africa that a historic declaration by the regional police emerged, calling the attention of their governments to the need to prioritize a regional strategy for combating illicit small arms proliferation in the SADC region. The general call for action led by SARPCCO was based on a simple tenet: without arms, the dynamics of conflict could not be served, but without arms reduction and control, the dynamics of peace could not be served, as attested to by the increase in armed crime and general armed violence, which often emerges immediately after a military conflict is overcome in Africa. Without the effective policing of arms—even if conflict is absent—the potential of arms to fuel human, national, and regional instability remains. In most cases of violence, arms are either directly or indirectly present, so most people are affected by arms in one way or another. And because the problem transcends borders, regional cooperation and coordination are fundamental to its solution.

Having identified regional cooperation and coordination as essential for action, governments started to focus on the capacity to implement a solution to the situation and the priority afforded such an implementation process at national levels. Disagreements emerged quickly and seemed to depend on how value systems affected individual perceptions of the threat posed by light weapons proliferation. Thus, for example, some countries were a "source" of weapons, others were seen as "end users," and a third type was merely important as "transit" countries. A general commitment to regional action had to be obtained first, regardless of how each member of the regional community saw the way it was being impacted by the problem nationally. Consensus was finally reached regionally when all countries accepted that although the impact was less in some than others, all were equally affected by the uncontrolled movement of illicit arms in and through the region. Once this was accepted, the region began to unpack a strategy for the sustainable management and reduction of this problem. The practical unpacking of the components of a strategy culminated in the legally binding SADC Protocol for the Control of Firearms, Ammunition, and Related Materials of 2001. The protocol served as inspiration for a Common African Approach on how to deal with the illicit trade in arms at the Organisation of African Unity (OAU) level and also served to inspire the African position in the United Nations Programme of Action on the Illicit Trade of Small Arms and Light Weapons in All its Aspects in July 2001.

IMPLEMENTING DEMOBILIZATION

Although the energy of the region was fundamentally spent on the legal frameworks and the enhancement of police activity for small arms control, the issue of improving reintegration schemes of demobilized soldiers was not forgotten. Foremost on the mind of the regional analysts was the case study of Angola, where two peacekeeping operations already had been scuttled largely due to lack of serious disarmament and demobilization. Indeed, the United Nations Angola Verification Mission (UNAVEM) II and UNAVEM III were classic cases of a failure in procedures and commitment that would eventually threaten the regional stability of southern Africa in the late 1990s. UNAVEM I demobilized foreign troops based on Angolan soil, namely South African and Cuban troops, and did not address any weapons issues or caches of weapons left behind. Still, given its limited mandate, it was successful. UNAVEM II focused on the cantonment rather than demobilization of Angolan warring parties, was poorly managed, did not include disarmament, and was neither comprehensive nor sustainable. After UNAVEM II failed, the mandate of UNAVEM III was not corrected and repeated the same mistakes as those of UNAVEM II.

UNAVEM II had neither the force nor the budget to ensure the monitoring that was required of it—it could not enforce compliance to any of the political or military processes mandated by the Bicesse peace agreement of 1991. Bicesse was supposed to produce a ceasefire, disarmament, the confinement and demobilizing of 152,000 armed forces of both warring parties, and the formation of a new 40,000–strong national army. Finally, it asked for multiparty elections. There was no disarmament and virtually no demobilization. The day after elections in 1992, only 8,000 troops reported for the formation of the new 40,000–strong national army. The country was at war within a month. After the Lusaka Protocol to the Bicesse Accords of 1994, a second opportunity for peace presented itself. This time the UN force was much stronger and more financially sound than before, and yet, despite the change in numbers and resources, the peace process unraveled from the start. Deployment was delayed, and the UN systematically turned a blind eye to acknowledged breaches of the protocol by both parties: "as the first combatants entered the assembly camps for disarmament and demobilization, as early as January 1995, it became clear that there was going to be little demobilization and almost no disarmament" (Cilliers and Dietrich 2000, 84). Angola was again at war in 1998.[2]

Lack of concerted demobilization and disarmament in the practical cases where it was attempted in southern Africa led to either the continuation of war or the rise of armed bandit groups. In the case of Angola, even in the years of "peace," entire combatant units that should have been demobilized and disarmed started to operate methodically in armed robbery of humanitarian convoys or in attacks against tourists crossing the border into Namibia and Zambia. Even when demobilization was more effective, as in the case of Mozambique, ex-combatants were paid past wages with guns that were then recycled into the illegal market. In the worst cases, those demobilized intelligence and logistics operators who were not taught new and employable skills quickly activated the old smuggling channels that had fed insurgency in the past and retooled these pipelines to serve the international criminal organizations moving goods and people between borders and continents.

Meanwhile, already active in its own reintegration, restructuring, and downsizing of military forces, South Africa commenced an approach by which demobilization could be undertaken without destabilizing transitional societies. But South Africa had not been in open war, as had been the case in Mozambique or Angola. The process in South Africa was focused on the legal and constitutional framework of military reform and the effort at consolidating a single, smaller, and integrated armed force that would serve the interests of the new South Africa. South Africa then focused on manners in which the reform of institutions, with particular reference to Security Sector Transformation, could assist in the consolidation of post-conflict societies and help to prevent the emergence of conflict situations in the future.

While countries like South Africa experimented with security reform and improvements in the entire criminal justice system as a key to development and reconstruction, they and other governments in the region, such as Botswana and Mozambique, focused their attention on prevention as well as management and resolution of conflict. It was clear that a general policy that would look at disarmament, demobilization, and economic development seriously was needed. It took three long years to obtain consensus of all heads of state in Africa, but the initial Omega and Millennium African Recovery Plan (MAP) for the reconstruction of Africa finally emerged in consolidated form as the NEPAD agenda agreed upon in Lusaka in 2001.

TOWARD AN INTEGRATED APPROACH TO DDR: AFRICA'S NEPAD INITIATIVE

THE MAKING OF A COMMON AFRICAN PEACE AND SECURITY AGENDA, 2001–2003

Since 2001 there has been a significant effort by African leaders to develop a road map for the regeneration of the continent in view of the enormous challenges facing Africa. This initiative has taken the form of the launching of the African Union in 2002 and the delineation of a blueprint for reconstruction of the continent in the form of the New Partnership for Africa's Development of 2001. Key in this blueprint is the acknowledgement that peace and security are essential preconditions for accelerated sustainable growth and development. To drive the process, a NEPAD Heads of State Implementation Committee (HSIC) and its Sub-Committee on Peace and Security, chaired by South Africa (in October 2001), were created. Since then enormous strides have been achieved in the establishment of an institutional framework and cultivation of political will to promote peace, security, and stability in Africa as a basis for the implementation of other NEPAD programs.

The most developed area for the relationship (both formal and informal) between NEPAD and the AU is around the peace and security agenda, defined as a core concern and a prerequisite for the implementation of all programs that seek the regeneration of Africa. Since the beginning of 2002, a concrete framework, that is continually being refined, has emerged for addressing matters of peace and security in and for Africa.

In March 2002 HSIC tasked South Africa, the chair of NEPAD's Sub-Committee on Peace and Security, to develop concrete steps for policy and program development in six areas identified as NEPAD priorities with respect to peace and security. These were (1) improvement of early warning capacity; (2) improvement of the capacity for, and coordination of, early action for conflict prevention, management, and resolution; (3) promotion of post-conflict reconstruction and development with a special focus on disarmament, demobilization, reintegration, and rehabilitation; (4) curbing of the illicit proliferation, circulation, and trafficking of small arms and light weapons on the continent; (5) promotion of democracy, good governance, and respect for human rights; and (6) assisting in resource mobilization for peace and security intervention in Africa.

In May 2002 the NEPAD Steering Committee endorsed these recommendations. These were presented to the HSIC, which crystallized them into the NEPAD Initial Action Plan at their meeting in Rome in June 2002. This plan formed the basis for the G8–Africa Action Plan adopted later that month in Kananaskis, Canada. After this, the NEPAD sub-committee took to developing concrete operational strategies for these broad areas, the first draft of which was created in July 2002.

By February 2003 this process had concretized into short-, medium-, and long-term activities in each priority area. These were presented, discussed, and consolidated into eight priority areas of the African Peace and Security Agenda (APSA) during the AU-NEPAD Consultation in Addis Ababa on February 17 and 18, 2003. It is critical to note that all six of NEPADs priority areas were adopted at part of APSA's eight priority areas for immediate action.

The final agreed APSA priorities were (1) developing mechanisms, institution-building processes, and support instruments for achieving peace and security in Africa; (2) improving capacity for, and coordination of, early action for conflict prevention, management, and resolution; (3) improving early warning capacity in Africa through strategic analysis and support; (4) prioritizing strategic security issues such as disarmament, demobilization, reintegration, reconciliation, and reconstruction and coordinating and ensuring effective implementation of African efforts aimed at preventing and combating terrorism;

(5) ensuring efficient and consolidated action for preventing, combating, and eradicating the problem of the illicit proliferation, circulation, and trafficking of small arms and light weapons; (6) improving the security sector and the capacity for good governance as related to peace and security; (7) generating minimum standards for application in the exploitation and management of Africa's resources (including nonrenewable resources) in areas affected by conflict; and (8) assisting in resource mobilization for the African Union Peace Fund and for regional initiatives aimed at preventing, managing, and resolving conflicts on the continent.[3]

As a way forward, the AU-NEPAD Consultation adopted three broad areas for immediate follow-up:

1. ensure regular information exchange between the AU Commission and the NEPAD Secretariat on all issues related to the AU-NEPAD peace and security initiative
2. schedule regular consultations on coordination and implementation of initiatives, elaborating strategies for the mobilization of resources and effective outreach initiatives to inform partners of the AU-NEPAD peace and security agenda
3. adoption by the AU Commission and the NEPAD Secretariat of more proactive approaches to addressing issues of peace and security on the continent; this included undertaking research on the root causes of conflicts and their prevention in Africa, the acceleration of capacity-building initiatives to address challenges to peace and security, and the utilization of African expertise in support of African initiatives.

The AU-NEPAD Consultation also considered the need to adopt a common approach to international peace and security partnership and developed proposals on how to approach such partnerships. Among them was the recommendation for the AU Commission and the NEPAD Secretariat to initiate contacts and provide joint presence and approaches with Africa's partners as part of a concerted effort to enlist support for the AU-NEPAD peace and security agenda.

The document of February 2003 was subsequently presented as AU-NEPAD priorities at the meeting of the G8[4] group with the NEPAD group in Berlin on March 6 and 7, 2003. In addition, the AU-NEPAD peace and security consultation report was endorsed by the Heads of States and Governments' Implementation Committee (HSGIC) meeting of the NEPAD Steering Committee in Abuja, Nigeria, on March 9, 2003, which welcomed the Addis Ababa AU-NEPAD Consultation meeting on peace and security of February 17 and 18, 2003, and endorsed its report. The HSGIC further encouraged the AU

Commission and NEPAD Secretariat to continue to work closely in promoting the AU Peace and Security agenda, to which the NEPAD is bringing added value.

In terms of operation, therefore, the envisaged framework is one where the AU and NEPAD are complementary and supportive of each other. This was clearly reflected in the Paris G8–Africa consultations of June 2003 and presented at the (G8 2003).

CHALLENGES TO THE
CONSOLIDATION OF THE AFRICAN INITIATIVE

Developing a common African agenda for peace and security has not been an easy process; neither has it been easy to convince all African heads of state that African structures needed a new vision and a new structure for direct action. It is therefore important to reflect on the challenges and the modes for the creation of consensus in Africa around these issues.

The principal challenges that the NEPAD initiative faces are both internal and external. Internal challenges can be reduced to three: the NEPAD initiative is considered a top-down initiative; it is a South African–led initiative; and it generates competition between existing agreed-upon African coordination structures and new NEPAD structures.

The harshest criticism of NEPAD in Africa is that it is a top-down initiative and does not have the buy-in of the African peoples, civil societies, or regional organizations. Ultimately, the strategy that originated the NEPAD initiative was led by a cluster of governments following South Africa's lead on the need to commence an "African Renaissance" process. Whatever the original criticisms internally and externally to the idea of a process of renaissance in the continent, the truth is that the idea of re-inventing oneself struck a very strong chord on a tired continent that was unable to step out of its internal problems to look at itself holistically. The idea was not fully developed at the time it was articulated, but the timing for the idea was right. Without a doubt the emergence of more democratic processes in key regions of Africa such as Nigeria, DRC, and South Africa, and the eventual electoral process in Kenya, introduced new ideas for the structuring of a continent-wide strategy for peace and development in the region. The additional attraction was the fact that it had a strong element of independence and pride posed by political leaders who had, in many cases, earned their wings after years of political and military struggle against different hegemonies.

The perception that NEPAD was a South African initiative is misplaced but continues to make the rounds, particularly in the academic circuits of Africa. This might be because the intelligentsia felt that they, rather than government officials, should have created the idea. It might also have originated through the coincidence of a change in administration in South Africa and the confusion surrounding Vice-President Mbeki's reflections on the need for an African Renaissance, which gained additional emphasis when he was elected president of South Africa. In any case, the NEPAD initiative was a Presidential Initiative supported by all heads of state of Africa from its inception, and it was managed by five countries on an equal basis in its steering committee form.

Rather than engaging NEPAD as a South African initiative, it can be said that initially competition over the ownership of both the AU and NEPAD ideas was particularly evident between northern and sub-Saharan Africa rather than between South Africa and the rest of the nations in the region. There also were divisions between eastern, western, and southern Africa in the process. The key to success in the ownership formula that lead to the signature in Lusaka was that NEPAD was not presented as a hard and fast plan but as a hard and fast idea. The framework for the ideal situation was easily agreed to as long as all those interested in leading the process would be allowed to make inputs into the construct of the components of NEPAD and its implementation.

The fact that the detail was left for later and that this detail would be consensually managed was fundamental for ownership. The other vital element was that countries should not immediately see in NEPAD a push for the integration of Africa. It is not the beginning of a "United States of Africa" or the beginning of common policies that will take away the individual power of states in the key areas of defense and economics. Rather, NEPAD was seen as and is a framework for cooperation based on the principle of all independent states of Africa visualizing a common minimum standard that can push the continent toward peace and prosperity. It is also very much the development of common positions vis-à-vis the international community, whether for the generation of common support for common causes or for the provision of a common framework for continental defense.

It follows that this type of thinking was nonthreatening to states as well as attractive to those who were seeking to restructure themselves or were in a process of transition out of conflict. The ones that were most threatened were those governments that benefited from the continuation of the status quo on the continent, but these were a minority that could not be seen as going against the wishes of the majority of their neighbors on the continent. It undoubtedly helped that NEPAD was not a donor-driven or foreign-led initiative since no one could dispute its independence from other influences.

The third challenge or misperception relating to the NEPAD initiative is that it threatens the normal run of existing African structures and competes with them. This perception was inevitable, given the ownership formula applied, which left the detail for later and concentrated on the idea first. Until such a time as the existing African structures were placed in their proper place in the order to come, and the ownership formula on the idea expanded to the intelligentsia and civil society, it follows that the most threatened were civil society and existing regional and continental structures. Civil society, but particularly nongovernmental organizations (NGOs), academics, and the private sector, considered NEPAD a political ploy—a feel-good mechanism that would never be implemented. NGOs, mostly responding to foreign-led initiatives that articulated a central role for civil society over and beyond governments, felt that NEPAD did not represent their interests. Academics were insulted in that the idea did not originate in a particular university, and the private sector was scared that this move would detract from profitable investment.

The truth is that since the NEPAD initiative was to be developed in substance after it was agreed upon on paper, the margins for interpretation as to what it ultimately would entail were very wide, and different sectors saw it in conjunction with different hopes and fears. The signature of NEPAD occurred at the same time that a decision was made to change the structure of the OAU to work toward an Africa Union. This was also seen as threatening by existing bureaucratic structures, who felt that they would be declared irrelevant and new bureaucracies set up in their stead. These two fears were particularly prevalent from September 2001 to September 2002, but these perceptions have now drastically changed.

Today, the concept and utility of NEPAD is more broadly recognized across all sectors, and the regional and continental organizations have already recognized the roles they will have to play in its implementation. The manner in which consensus was reached against the above-mentioned adversity had to do with two decisions: the creation of specialized committees of personal representatives of heads of state representative of all regions; and the creation of an agenda for multiple meetings to provide a direct role to at least twenty African countries in the construction of the detail. The different committees on policy and governance, peace and security, and economic development were led by different countries working in tandem, with all their decisions reviewed and ratified by heads of state meeting on a regular basis, many times a year.

The transparency between the NEPAD Secretariat set up in South Africa and the OAU Secretariat first and the AU Commission later also assisted in keeping all stakeholders abreast of the changes. The sheer volume of work and energy needed to deal with the most difficult questions of the NEPAD formula impressed upon all those connected to the process a feeling of determination. This in turn led the few sceptics to see in NEPAD not only a promise but a workable formula for sustained action in Africa, by Africans and for Africans. The force became irresistible.

The external challenges to NEPAD were ultimately resolved in a similar manner. Initially, the donor and the international communities saw in NEPAD and the AU only a change of name rather than a change in direction. In effect, they feared that this was a new political ploy to generate donor interest but that no real reform would follow. The fact that the NEPAD initiative was able to advance so quickly into the development of operational guidelines for action surprised the international community. This is expressly recognized, for example, in the G8–Africa discussions that have taken place since the G8–NEPAD meeting of Kananaskas, Canada, in 2002. Between Kananaskas and Evian, African countries had promised and delivered a number of key policies: the unpacking of the African Peer Review Mechanism; the creation of a Common African Defense and Security Policy; the AU Peace and Security Council Protocol; and the common agenda for AU-NEPAD peace and security action. Furthermore, individually and collectively, efforts at brokering peace in Africa by Africans also took a turn for the better with relative successes in Angola, Ethiopia, Eritrea, Sierra Leone, DRC, Burundi, Rwanda, Sudan, and Côte D'Ivoire. Democracy also became consolidated in key countries, particularly in Kenya. More importantly, the African countries were seen to talk in one voice on issues of partnership with the donor community behind the AU-NEPAD agenda. All of this has served to reduce the suspicion on the ultimate fate of NEPAD.

Perhaps the biggest tension of all was between the AU Commission and African organizations restructured for service action. The AU-NEPAD consultations, which took a year to create, ultimately bore fruit in February 2003, and a single common agenda has emerged. The challenge now is to keep momentum and to implement action on the one hand and revitalize and strengthen the subregional organizations that need to prevent, manage, and reduce conflict in Africa on the other hand. This is why its pays to understand the thinking behind the NEPAD initiative.

UNDERSTANDING THE AU-NEPAD THINKING ON APSA

The New Partnership for Africa's Development asserts that peace, security, democracy, good governance, human rights, and sound economic management are conditions for sustainable development. Regarding peace and security, there is one overarching priority: preventing, managing, and resolving violent conflict in Africa.

The effective prevention, management, and resolution of conflicts in Africa is needed to reduce the loss of life, the displacement of people, and the destruction of infrastructure and property, thereby generating a stable environment that will greatly enhance economic activity and attract investment, which will assist in the eradication of poverty. A commitment by Africans and the international community to thoroughly analyze the fundamental causes of conflict will significantly increase the effectiveness of the proposed interventions.

The following principles underpin the NEPAD Peace and Security Programme:

- it must be led by Africans
- the international community must support peace and security efforts in Africa
- the African Union and the Regional Economic Communities (RECs), such as SADC, EAC, IGAD, ECOWAS, and ECCAS,[5] must form a single continental architecture for peace and security
- prevention of conflict is preferable to its management and resolution
- active participation and involvement of AU member states in peace and security matters is key

The proposed NEPAD Peace and Security Programme comprises a holistic process that is designed to provide sustainable capability to African states and regional and continental organizations to prevent, manage, and resolve conflict.

The rationale for this program lies in the belief that the prevention of conflict is preferable to its management and resolution. Prevention is the most cost effective option, not only in terms of the costs of peacemaking but also because of the losses in economic, human, social, and political capital that accompany conflict. Conflict prevention, management, and resolution will entail a long-term process focused on enhancing the capacity of subregional and regional organizations to reduce the incidence of, and mitigate the effects of, conflict on the continent.

For these reasons, the focus of action across the initial six priority areas of the NEPAD Peace and Security Programme revolved around the concept of improved information and analysis; ensuring that early warning leads to early and effective action; and promoting sustainable disarmament, demobilization, and post-conflict reconstruction initiatives that promote a culture of peace and justice in and for Africa. Fundamental to all of these issues was the urgent need to improve the administration, capacity, coordination, and information exchange between and among Africans behind a single objective. Resource mobilization was also important as it impacted independence and sustainability of long-term efforts.

For the NEPAD program, peace and security is about people. When societies emerge from wars that have lasted for decades, it is not only the former armed combatants whose needs must be addressed. The devastation of war affects the society as a whole, including communities and displaced persons and refugees, and, therefore, the healing processes must be designed to address the needs of the whole of such societies. For this reason, post-conflict disarmament, demobilization, rehabilitation, and reintegration (DDRR) must not be conceived of as a process focused solely on implementation in the military context. DDRR must also take into consideration issues of reconciliation and development, and post-conflict requirements must be taken into account when the conflict is still being resolved—not later. For this same reason, the area of disarmament, for example, not only takes into account arms that were in the possession of warring parties but also—through the initiative to prevent, combat, and eradicate the illicit trade in small arms and light weapons, which is another fundamental pillar of NEPAD—those in the possession of civilians and outside of the control of organized structures.

An interesting issue that emerged in the NEPAD discussion of DDR needs is that the concept of DDR itself was not an Africa originated, led, or endorsed concept. Since 1999 the international donor and relief community has been discussing the issue of DDR as part of a corrective measure from lessons emerging from large multinational peace support operations such as those in Cambodia, the former Yugoslav Republic, and Central America. Lack of coordination, however, raised raised two problems: peacekeeping often required demobilization with little or no mention of effective disarmament, and there was a lack of interest in post-peace reintegration of ex-combatants.

As a result of a variety of pressures, such as those present in the Brahimi Report[6] for the improvement of peacekeeping operations, the international and relief communities commenced to present peace support operations and post-conflict reconstruction needs revolving around the integrated concept of disarmament, demobilization, and reintegration. In Africa these conceptual issues had not been developed along the same lines. There also had been little focus on disarmament and demobilization planning and implementation needs during the brokering of peace agreements. At most, Africa had looked at the issues of political settlement, demobilization, and the end of armed opposition rather than the physical needs of disarming and demobilizing. In contrast, however, there had been much more attention to stabilizing post-conflict governments through a number of more indigenous strategies, such as those of reconciliation between ex-combatants and between ex-combatants and the population at large.

Equally, since many of the combatants had been children, there was a strong interest in the rehabilitation of child soldiers, including girl soldiers. This was the same principle that applied to people who had been injured due to armed conflict because the number of disabled war veterans on either side was very large. Rehabilitation also indicated this aspect of the African thinking. Finally, reintegration, highest on the agenda, for years had mostly referred to the generation of a unique national defense organization that would be retooled to include ex-combatants from different warring parties. These needed to be integrated into a national body.

It was thus that, little by little, the concept of reintegration usually mentioned by the donor and relief community as one where ex-soldiers were reintegrated to civilian communities was enlarged to include all aspects of the post-conflict transition in the country at large: reintegration, rehabilitation, and reconciliation. These three dimensions ensured the political, physical, emotional, and economic resolution of deep socioeconomic problems emerging from decades of conflict. Ultimately, the last "R" in the African debate was always deemed to be that of "Reconstruction" of the nation after conflict had ended.

As NEPAD focused on the issue of DDR, it was perhaps unavoidable that a concept that was considered as serving the needs of multinational agencies rather than the real needs of the emerging countries themselves would emerge. The original debates of donor and relief agencies, including the UN system, about the need to focus on demobilization, disarmament, and reintegration of ex-combatants, and to tie these elements to post-conflict reconstruction, were perceived to be connected with conflict resolution measures: ultimately, an exit point at the end of a peace process. As the discussion of post-conflict reconstruction emerged in Africa in the last two years, the nature of the problem for Africa in particular began to change the perception of what classical DDR stands for. Here, the APSA priorities began to identify African DDR needs as being much more complex than those visualized by the international community. It is not just about demobilization of warring parties and their disarmament and reintegration. DDR really should reach out to the demilitarization and disarmament of a population and an infrastructure that had been mobilized and prepared to sustain war for decades. In order to generate post-conflict constructs, elements of national reconciliation and economic reconstruction had to be added. Finally, due to the extent of psychological and physical trauma on warring parties and civilians at the end of conflict, the problem of rehabilitation had to be considered and addressed. This is why in the APSA priorities of the AU-NEPAD agenda the concept of "DDR" has been changed to that of "DDRR," with the last "R" representing variables such as Reintegration, Rehabilitation, Reconciliation, and national Reconstruction.

Other key elements that emerge throughout the NEPAD Peace and Security Programme are those that relate to strengthening national, regional, and continental governance and action processes. The stronger the capacity, coordination, and governance at national level, the stronger the regional secretariats will be to engage in early warning, early action, and post-conflict reconstruction. Similarly, the stronger the regional secretariats are, the stronger the ability of continental organizations to assist and support continental peace, security, and governance processes. The NEPAD Capacity Building Programme seeks to address capacity deficiencies of governments, including in the area of peace and security.

African governments must support their own national, regional, and continental processes and not rely entirely on funds from abroad. This is fundamental to ensuring the holistic approach to peace and security in Africa. When considering the role of the international community in assisting the promotion of peace and security in Africa, assistance must be aligned to real African needs in a spirit of new partnership. This new partnership between Africa and the international community should be at three levels: principle, dialogue, and administration. Innovative methods should be sought for effective action that will bring together governments, the private sector, and civil society.

The 2002 objective of the new Africa Union structures was to unpack and develop policy surrounding the principal pillars of African security, as follows:

- undertake policy and institutional reform of the security sector as a whole so as to promote democracy and respect for human rights; undertake a process to govern the management of nonrenewable resource exploitation in African regions affected by conflict with a view to reduce illicit and criminal behavior and enhance governance and development
- promote debate, define components, and secure action for disarmament and demobilization initiatives that extend to rehabilitation, reintegration, reconciliation, and reconstruction in post-conflict situations
- consolidate the African and international initiatives to curb the proliferation of illicit small arms in Africa and promote the creation of sustainable national and regional plans of action for arms management and disarmament in Africa.

NEPAD also focused on the implementing agencies and their capacity to deliver on these objectives. For that reason the most interesting developments of the new Africa Union during 2002–03 were the creation of the Peace and Security Council, the Military Staff Committee, and the African Stand-by Force (which was first mandated to come up with a common defense policy for African Armed Forces regarding professionalism and training) and the new conflict prevention and management divisions that coordinate peace support operations, humanitarian and disaster relief operations, and mustering of the assistance needed for post-conflict reconstruction from the developmental perspective. A further key to this initiative is the fact that not only were objectives clearly identified, but an implementing structure has been proposed that relies on implementation by subregional organizations assisted by a central coordinating body within the AU Commission.

Finally, NEPAD has three fundamental pillars: peace and security, governance and democracy, and economic development. This demonstrates that the concept of security and development has been promoted in Africa to take into account all the lessons learned in the past attempts at peace generation and post-conflict reconstruction.

Conclusion

Post-agreement demobilization, disarmament, and reintegration is one of the major pillars upon which conflict-affected states can organize themselves and generate sustainable post-conflict reconstruction. Most of the lessons learned on these three items have come from foreign literature based on information gathered by international peace support agencies, international relief agencies, or the donor community. Seldom has the information come from the people that were affected by imperfect demobilization, disarmament, and reintegration. There is a great need for us to be able to look at these three elements from the point of view of the directly impacted and his/her society as a whole.

Ideas about how to correct DDR are still mostly based on international perspectives and economic imperatives rather than the experiences of those in areas where DDR was implemented. And yet what we are seeing in Africa is that a total change of the paradigm of DDR is emerging. The concept has not only been enlarged but has shifted focus. Whereas the international community considers DDR as a conflict resolution mechanism at the end of a process, Africa considers DDRR as a conflict prevention mechanism at the beginning of a process. This will naturally require a different approach to its implementation.

To sum up, a new thinking about DDR is emerging in Africa and is contained under both the NEPAD initiative and the structures that are being put in place to implement this vision, under the AU Commission and the subregional organizations that exist in Africa. Fundamental to this vision is a great truth that lies at the bottom of all effective DDR: the chances for success of peace-making and post-conflict reconstruction are exponentially increased if there is a regional umbrella of states immediately surrounding the affected state that is united and willing to take part in a constructive manner in the implementation of peace. This is not only true for Africa. Affected states in the Americas, in Europe or in Asia have more chances to prosper if there is a regional support umbrella that operates with a minimum regional standard and with one voice in assisting peace and reconstruction in that country.

Aside from the need to construct regional umbrellas and fora in support of a common approach to peace and DDR, there is also a need to consider DDR in a broader and more long-term light than previously. In Africa, DDR itself is now unpacked differently, comprising not just ex-combatants but the whole process of reconciliation, rehabilitation, and reintegration as well as reconstruction, affecting not just warriors but the victims of violence and society in general. Similarly, disarmament of ex-combatants is balanced out through preventing, combating, and eradicating of the illicit trade in small arms and light weapons. This is an important variation since traditional DDR only focuses on weapons in possession of a legal combatant and not in the hands of civilians, bandits, or criminals who operate in and out of borders.

In addition, DDR should also be seen as only one component of a longer and more comprehensive process. In Africa, under NEPAD, DDR is seen as one of eight: improved bureaucratic structures for coordinated action; improved early warning capability from the subregion itself; early action capacity (including peace support capabilities) for conflict prevention, management, and resolution; managing and reducing the cross-border trade in illicit arms; generating minimum standards for the operations of private corporations and ensuring sharing of resources in relation to the exploitation of Africa's natural resources; security sector reform; and having the ability to manage and create resources to sustain action. Ultimately DDR is the first step in construction of the new order, rather than the last step of something that has ceased to be.

By ensuring a broader definition of DDR, providing a regional umbrella to support its implementation, and balancing DDR with other key elements in post-conflict reconstruction, an effective road-map for sustainable peace can be developed and conflict prevention applied. The beauty of this approach is that, if it were taken early enough, it can also form part of the terms and conditions that warring parties must agree to in the pursuit of a lasting peace agreement in the first place. They will then be effectively contributing to the prevention of renewed conflict and helping to secure sustainable development.

NOTES

1. UNIDIR produced eleven publications with case studies on the nature of peacekeeping operations since 1989 (UNIDIR 1996–98); the United Nations has also published all the material related to their peacekeeping operations in their blue book series, and extensive publications worldwide have analyzed the nature of success or failure in a multinational support operation.

2. Since 2002, with the death of UNITA commander Jonas Savimbi, there has been a third chance at peace in Angola. Although cantonment started in May 2002, many of the soldiers earmarked for demobilization have left their camps due to lack of food and resources since no reintegration and retraining program has yet been put in place by the government.

3. For a comprehensive discussion, refer to the report of the AU-NEPAD Consultations on Peace and Security (available online at www.saferafrica.org).

4. The G8 is a grouping of industrialized countries comprised of the United States, France, the United Kingdom, Russia, China, Japan, Italy, and Canada. At the G8 Summit of every year, there is now a session where the G8 and the NEPAD Steering Committee countries meet to discuss partnerships and needs. The first such session was developed at Kananaskas, Canada, in 2002 and the second at Evian, France, in 2003. The AU-NEPAD agenda now includes a process of consultation in preparation for the G8–NEPAD consultations; two meetings were held (in Berlin and Paris) in 2002 and 2003 in preparation for the meeting in Evian. The APSA agenda and its needs are discussed in this forum.

5. Southern African Development Community, East African Community, West African Economic Community, Central African Economic Community.

6. The Brahimi Report (Brahimi 2000) was a UN-mandated commission that looked at the failures of peace support operations after the end of UNPROFOR in Bosnia and Herzegovina. Led by Ambassador Brahimi, it looked at all UN peace support operations and analyzed their failure to achieve objectives, particularly in relation to protection of civilian populations, disarmament, and demobilization. Many of the findings and recommendations of the Brahimi Report had already been identified in the UNIDIR Disarmament and Conflict Resolution (DRC) series of 1994–95. All of this led to UN recommendations that changed the scope, focus, and manner in which UN peace support operations could engage, as seen in East Timor and in subsequent operations.

Dominic Murray

Post-Accord Police Reform

History teaches us that effective reform of security forces in general, and of police in particular, is perhaps the most important factor in determining the relative success of post-accord peace processes. It is important to note regarding such reform that the needs of countries in transition are likely to be both context specific and multilayered. Kelly (1995) describes policing in Haiti under the old regime as an unchecked instrument of state oppression, indistinguishable from the military and with no tradition of police service. A United Nations report accused the police and armed forces in Guatemala of cold-blooded murder and running death squads to kill common thieves, drug traffickers, car thieves, etc. These hardly compare, in substance if not importance, with the policing in Northern Ireland, where the motivation for police reform stems more from the perception that governance as a state monopoly should be questioned and reviewed.

These differing contexts and reform needs have become more apparent during the final quarter of the twentieth century as intrastate conflicts became much more common than wars between states. In this regard, Holm and Eide (2000) contend that peace settlements following interstate wars have tended to address the specific reason for the dispute, for instance, control over a contested territory. In contrast, peace settlements following intrastate conflicts in many cases require a complete regeneration of the core functions of society and government; thus a peace accord is not so much the end product as a milestone on the long road to a sustainable peace.

Obviously, as the nature of conflicts changes, so also will the attempts to resolve them. Most attempts at conflict resolution, perhaps, share the need for

- increased acceptability and trust
- increased transparency and accountability
- increased professionalism

Stanley and Call (2003) contend that the long-term stability of post–civil war regimes, particularly those based on liberal democratic models, depends on institutional arrangements that minimize the likelihood that organized coercive forces will intervene in politics. Few would argue with the claim that, for a police service to operate effectively, it should reflect the values and culture of the society that it serves. The problem here is that in conflict situations, society often consists of conflicting communities with police serving one (often elite) section only. Nonetheless, Huntington (1992) records that between 1974 and 1991 more than thirty countries in southern Europe, Latin America, East Asia, and Eastern Europe shifted from authoritarian to democratic systems of government. There have been many attempts since then that have ranged from the internal reform of policing in South Africa to the activities of the United Nations Civil Police (UNCIVPOL) in Kosovo. In the former, a fair degree of success was achieved despite the fact that the "new" South Africa had the unenviable task of reforming a police force of close to 140,000 officers who hitherto had been involved in the implementation and defense of apartheid. Between 1994 and 1999 more than 22,000 former liberation fighters and black homeland soldiers were integrated into the military. The civilianization of the new South African Police Service (SAPS) was aided by the implementation of an independent Complaints Commission. The ultimate objective of the reforms is the introduction of a culture of community policing. All of this was made possible largely due to a strong government commitment and clear focus of power, both of which are lacking in Kosovo, which has necessitated the UN taking much more direct responsibility for policing there than in their other operations.

Conflict theorists have frequently argued that differences in economic resources give elites the ability to control the coercive apparatus of the state. Obviously, these elites have a strong motivation to maintain order so that ongoing relationships will not be disturbed. Jacobs (1979) employed this argument in the context of differential socioeconomic positioning, but it can be just as appropriately applied to post-conflict political accords. This is particularly so when the nature of the state itself is at issue. Darby (2000) has argued that governments are often divided about peace processes, and governmental or quasi-governmental agencies may continue covert actions to undermine the process. The lack of a clear and unified state approach to police reform, for example, may cause disaffection within the security forces, which has the potential to undermine the peace process itself. Bayley is rather more outspoken: "If the indigenous government is hostile to the democratic reform of policing, go home!" (1997, 103). He goes on to argue that the police cannot be an instrument of reform because unless a government is committed to democracy, reform of the police can do little to bring it about. Nevertheless, since a strong (and loyal) police force is the most direct way to maintain order, it is likely to be the most important factor in any process that seeks change in a nation's government. It is hardly surprising, therefore, that an essential element of most peace accords is the reform of state security, including policing.

Generally, the reform of security forces as a part of peace accords has tended to take two forms. These have been variously referred to as "military merger" and "demilitarization and police reform." The first implies that integrating former enemy armies into one another is necessary to establish security guarantees among parties to the conflict. In El Salvador the peace accord produced the compromise that the police force was disbanded and a new force created consisting of former Farabundo Marti National Liberation Front (FMLN) fighters (20 percent), former security forces (20 percent), and civilians (60 percent). In Namibia, the Peoples Liberation Army and the Southwest Africa Territorial Force were merged into a national defense force.

The second form attempts to shift the bulk of interior security responsibilities to a reformed civilian police force. In Mozambique for example, in accordance with the 1990 constitution, the former Police of the Republic of Mozambique (PRM) was developed under a clear directive to depoliticize and restructure policing in the country. Since democratization in Nigeria, attempts to demilitarize policing have included the gradual official recognition and inclusion of regional/ethnic vigilante organizations (Yoruba, Hausa, Igbo) that had existed previously to fight the excesses of the military. The implementation of the Palestinian Authority in the Middle East seems to be drawn from both merger and reform models. Under the Oslo Accord, Israel decided to reach a settlement with the Palestinian Liberation Organization (PLO) on the understanding that violence from and within the Occupied Territories would cease if the PLO were permitted to take responsibility for their own internal security.

Holm and Eide (2000) argue that the extent to which a post-conflict community can establish a security sector that is legitimate and loyal to the new state structures may be the key to the success or failure of any peace accord. In this regard, it would seem that the military merger option has the advantage of being highly visible and perhaps providing at least short-term satisfaction of demands. By its very nature, however, reform of existing police structures is likely to require a cascade of innovations ranging from respect for human rights to transparency and accountability. The most important factors in all of this are likely to be the nature and range of training procedures for emerging police structures, and these are likely to take time. Malan (2000) claims that in Mozambique, five years after the 1990 constitution, the functions, personnel, structures, and operational procedures of the police remained in need of comprehensive reform. Often, post-conflict accords come under pressure due to inflated expectations of changes in policing and a reluctance to accept that change takes time. In peace processes gradualism may have long-term benefits with a short-term price to pay.

As with the application of all models to human behavior, caution is required. In the context of police reform, we should be careful when using terms like "implementation." For example, Northern Ireland is often cited as an instance where police reform has been implemented, and in one sense it has. However, one section of the population there would argue that the reforms have been much too sweeping, while others would claim that they have neither gone far enough nor fast enough. This suggests that structural reform of policing is doomed to fail in the absence of concomitant attitudinal change. This raises the important question of how measures of police reform are perceived by those actually involved in the post-conflict situation.

Perhaps the most important element in the reform of any police force is the concept of trust. This is vital within the police both in the context of cuts in personnel, which normally reflect the lessening of a previous security threat, and recruitment, which would ensure that the composition of the new police force is representative of the population as a whole. The public perception of the police in terms of aspects such as fairness, transparency, and effectiveness is also of vital concern. Indeed, the most significant factors in determining the success or failure of any post-accord peace process are the degree to which police officers accept the changes that are often imposed upon them and the public perception of the ability of the emerging service to maintain security in an evenhanded way. Consensus rarely exists in this regard. Nonetheless, as Lord Scarman remarked, "the success of policing operations depends in the last resort, not upon questions of technique or professional expertise, but upon the degree of confidence felt by society in its police" (Scarman Commission, 1969, 69).

Often overt and tangible cues are required to nurture such confidence. When new policing institutions are created, or when important new changes are introduced, different symbols and name changes are often designed to reflect the spirit of the reforms. The attempt to emphasis the civilian nature of the new Autonomous Police in the Basque Country in 1981 is an example. The name of the new police, the "Ertzaintza," means "shepherd of the people" and historically was the name of local Basque police; the new name coincided with a change of uniform. The creation of the unarmed An Garda Siochana (guardians of the peace) in the Republic of Ireland in 1922 is another example of a state taking steps to eschew its militaristic past.

What is clear is that police reform has taken many different forms in the various contexts in which it has taken place. As stated previously, it has tended to be both multifaceted and context specific. Therefore, the complexities of reform might best be appreciated through reference to particular cases. The cases considered here are of the development and post-conflict attempts to solve the "police problem" in Northern Ireland and Serbia and Montenegro.

Northern Ireland

The State of Northern Ireland was brought into being by the Government of Ireland Act (1920), which partitioned the country and provided for two parliaments, one in Dublin and one in Belfast. Despite the ongoing and extremely violent Anglo-Irish war being fought between British forces and Irish Volunteers (later known as the Irish Republican Army or IRA) mainly but not wholly in the southern part of the country, a new parliament for Northern Ireland was opened in Belfast on June 22, 1921. Shortly after this, on July 9, a truce was agreed upon between London and the IRA, followed by the signing of an Anglo-Irish Treaty in London on December 6, 1921. The treaty accepted the reality of the partition of the country. For one section of the Irish population this represented an enormous betrayal, and very quickly a vicious civil war between pro- and anti-treaty factions began, which lasted until April 1923.

The whole period was one of great uncertainty and instability in all parts of the island of Ireland. In the north, the newly elected unionist government was faced with regular sectarian rioting within its own borders (for example, the violent expulsion of Catholics from the Belfast shipyards) and continuing attacks from the IRA both internally and across its new border with the south, leading to further unrest and disruption. The new unionist state of Northern Ireland felt itself under threat from the south, which still laid claim to the north, and from a significant Catholic minority within its borders, who neither identified with, nor accepted, the new arrangements. To help counter this threat and to bring the various irregular vigilante groups under control, the Ulster Special Constabulary was formed. The membership of this force was drawn exclusively from the Protestant community.

The Royal Ulster Constabulary (RUC) was formed in 1922 when responsibility for internal security was devolved from Westminster to Belfast. It was centralized and under direct political control, with the Inspector General answerable to the Unionist Minister of Home Affairs in the Northern Irish Government. He commanded a police force of 3,000, backed up by the part-time B Special Force. It was intended initially that Catholics would comprise one-third of the new force, representing the proportion of Catholics in the population of the new region. Not for the last time in Northern Ireland, this aspiration was not fulfilled. Catholic representation peaked at 21 percent in 1923, fell to 17 percent by 1927, and was 10 percent by the outbreak of the present round of conflict in 1969.

From the beginning the RUC was an armed force. Its role was clearly a political one and seen primarily as defending the state against attacks from the IRA and similar antipartition groups. The minority Catholic community as a whole was also perceived to be essentially disloyal and antagonistic to the police. The government made little attempt to attract the support of the Catholic community. As a result, a kind of self-fulfilling prophecy seemed to operate, with many nationalists feeling obliged to accept the role to which they had been assigned.

To assist the police in their perceived role as defenders of the state, in 1922 the government passed a "Special Powers Act," which gave wide powers of search and arrest and allowed internment without trial, suspension of inquests, and the imposition of curfews. An inquiry into policing by the British National Council for Civil Liberties in 1936 was critical of the RUC's political role. It reported that the police did not act impartially when dealing with marches or protests and consistently favored Protestants at the expense of Catholics.

The authority of the unionist government was not seriously challenged until the civil rights protests began in 1968. From the beginning, the leaders of this campaign emphasized that they were not opposing the existence of the government but were looking for the establishment of British patterns of social justice within the governance of Northern Ireland. However, there was a tendency to brand the civil rights leaders as antipartitionists whose real agenda was to destroy the state. The state's first line of defense was inevitably the RUC, with the result that the series of civil rights marches during 1968 and 1969 in Dungannon, Belfast, Armagh, and Londonderry were treated by the police as attacks on the state. The subsequent policing of the disturbances exposed the failure of the police to act impartially. Bardon writes: "Images of unrestrained police batoning unarmed demonstrators including MPs, 'without justification or excuse,' as the Cameron Commission judged later, flashed across the world" (1992, 674).

The rioting that followed the march in Londonderry in August 1969 spread to Belfast and other areas, until it was evident that the police could no longer control the situation. As a result the British army was called in, in support of the police, and assumed a control of the security operations that lasted for the next eight years, with the police playing a secondary role. A committee led by Lord Hunt investigated the policing of the disturbances. Hunt's recommendations included the disarming of the police, the repeal of the Special Powers Act, the disbandment of the Ulster Special Constabulary, and the establishment of a Police Authority of Northern Ireland.

The civilianization of the police force proposed by Hunt was almost immediately undermined by the emergence of the Provisional IRA and a deteriorating security situation. Within a few weeks the police had to be rearmed, and a new RUC Reserve Force was created to assist the police in controlling civil disturbances. The Ulster Defence Regiment was formed in 1970 to patrol borders and protect the state; many of its members were recruited from the disbanded Ulster Special Force (B Specials). The Special Powers Act was replaced by the Emergency Provisions Act (1973) and reinforced by the Prevention of Terrorism Act (1974). These gave the police greater powers than they had enjoyed under the old Special Powers Act. They suspended the right to jury trial, reintroduced internment, and gave the police wider powers of arrest.

Following the Hunt Report, the Police Act (1970) established an independent Police Authority for Northern Ireland as a means of increasing police accountability to the public and to distance the police from political control. In theory the act gave the Police Authority important powers over the police, but in a deteriorating security situation these powers were never effectively applied. By 1971 the IRA had gone on the offensive with a bombing campaign all over Northern Ireland. The reintroduction of internment without trial by the Faulkner government in 1972, followed by allegations of ill treatment of internees and the shooting dead of thirteen civilians by British paratroopers at a civil rights demonstration in Derry (Bloody Sunday), served to increase recruitment to the Provisional IRA. A number of vigilante groups were policing both communities, and there was pressure from unionist ranks for a "third force" to defeat the IRA. In March 1972 the Northern Ireland parliament was dissolved and direct rule imposed from Westminster.

After 1969 the RUC, in practice, assisted the army, whose security policy was generally governed by reaction to events. The army's strategy was a military one, and the ongoing conflict resulted in fortification of police stations and further militarization of the police. Complaints about ill treatment of prisoners by police were investigated and reported upon by Amnesty International in 1978. They found sufficient evidence of maltreatment of suspected terrorists to warrant a public inquiry.

By 1976 the policy of police primacy was recognized as "the way ahead," and the RUC resumed a central role in policing. The new chief constable saw his tasks as restoring the police to a central role, developing a counterinsurgency strategy, and enshrining impartiality as a guiding principle of the police force. Events on the street undermined this ideal. The RUC was under attack from all sides, and normal policing at this time was simply not an option. For their own protection, the police had to be armed and had to travel in heavily armored vehicles. The Police Federation protested increasingly that the use of a civil police force for military duty was inappropriate. Nevertheless, on January 1, 1977, the new policy of police primacy was firmly established under a joint directive signed by the military commander and the chief constable. Meanwhile, increasingly successful operations against Protestant paramilitaries, and the policing of banned orange (Protestant) parades and demonstrations, weakened the heretofore conviction that the RUC was their (Protestants') police service. The police were confused, attacked from all sides, and racked by allegations of shoot-to-kill policies and collusion with loyalist groups. By the end of 1998, 302 police men and women had been killed and thousands maimed and injured.

Eventually, in April 1998 the majority of the political parties in Northern Ireland signed the Good Friday Agreement. The difficult and contentious issue of policing was an important element within the agreement, and it was agreed that an independent commission on policing would be set up. This was quickly put in place under the chairmanship of Chris Patten, and it was charged with making recommendations for a future police service that would be professional, effective and efficient, fair and impartial, free from partisan political control; accountable both under the law for its actions and to the community it serves; representative of the society it polices and operates within a coherent and cooperative criminal justice system, which conforms with human rights norms.

The key changes recommended in the commission's final report included a new name and symbols for the police service, a new Policing Board to replace the current Police Authority, comprehensive action to focus policing on human rights, new District Policing Partnership Boards to carry out local consultation on policing, and unique arrangements for recruitment designed to redress religious imbalances in the composition of the police service. The secretary of state is responsible for producing long-term objectives and principles. The chief constable has operational responsibility and also has an obligation to report to the Policing Board. The board will hold the chief constable and the Police Service to account, negotiate a budget, and present an annual policing plan. The Police Board is also responsible for appointing the chief constable, subject to the approval of the secretary of state. The board may follow up any report from the chief constable by instigating an inquiry by the ombudsman, Her Majesty's Inspector of Constabulary, or the Audit Office.

It has been stated previously that changes in structure alone are unlikely to produce lasting or effective police reform. It also has been suggested that successful reform is likely to be multifaceted in nature. A graphic example of this is that the Patten Commission recommended no less than 175 changes in policing in Northern Ireland. These are discussed here under five general headings.

CULTURE

In the Patten Report (1999) the general notion of organizational culture is defined as the way in which an organization sees itself and manages itself internally and the way in which it sees and interacts with its clients and others outside the organization. In the context of police reform, Cramphorn laid considerable emphasis on culture, stressing what he clearly perceived to be its all-encompassing importance: "Culture is far more important in determining whether policing is congruent with the values of community than are accountability techniques per se or the organizational structures of the police. This is because culture informs all police activity" (Cramphorn 2001).

Few would argue with the claim that, for a police service to operate effectively, it should reflect the values and culture of the community that it serves. The problem for the Royal Ulster Constabulary was that traditionally its relative effectiveness was determined by an identity with the culture of only one section of the community. The changes in policing in Northern Ireland consequent upon the Good Friday Agreement are obviously of considerable importance in this regard. The Patten Report initiated a considerable debate about all aspects of policing, and the name of the force has changed from the "Royal Ulster Constabulary" to the "Police Service of Northern Ireland" (PSNI). An important element in the decision to change the name was that, along with other aspects of the peace process, the new name would signal a change in the relationship between the force and the community as a whole. The badge emblem of the force was also changed, and the Union flag was removed from police stations. It should be remembered that symbols tend to carry a significance far beyond their objective selves. The proposed changes engendered more opposition from unionists than any other section of the Patten Report. They were perceived as a betrayal of the memory of "their" police.

There appear to have been three issues affecting the degree of communication or interaction between the RUC and the community. The first is the culture of secrecy that exists within most police services, where information and its protection is often a crucial element in the success or failure of their activities. Second, the force traditionally identified with, and perhaps related to, one section of the community only. Third was the existence of the Special Branch—described by Patten as a force within a force—which was not only distant from the community but also from other officers who were ignorant (and on occasions fearful) of its activities. It is probable, however, that there will always be a tension between a perceived need for secrecy and a demand for transparency. This is likely to be most marked in post-conflict situations where information may be held on "ex-terrorists" who may now be applying to join the new police service or actually hold places in government.

ACCOUNTABILITY

It is accepted that modern policing should be based on a culture of accountability. However, the concept of accountability is a complex one. For example, human rights law requires police to balance competing, and sometimes conflicting, rights. To do so they must exercise discretion. This may lead to selective under-enforcement, which may be discriminatory or perceived to be so. But it certainly makes accountability uncertain. In Northern Ireland there are particular problems in this regard, such as the conflicting claims of marchers and residents.

Prior to the establishment of a new Policing Board, the RUC was accountable to the secretary of state through the Police Authority of Northern Ireland. The Police Authority, however, lacked total autonomy because its members were appointed and could be dismissed by the secretary of state. Although the authority could ask the chief constable to produce specific reports, these could be, and often were, refused. This apparent lack of accountability had a number of important side effects. When a number of murders and assassinations occurred, claims were made that the security forces had colluded with loyalist paramilitaries. Accusations of this sort had rarely been independently investigated. The result was a diminution of confidence in the original Police Authority and a dangerous loss of confidence in the RUC within some parts of the community.

Such events undoubtedly influenced the Patten Report recommendations and led to the emergence of proposed initiatives designed to optimize police accountability in Northern Ireland. A new Policing Board was established with nineteen members, ten of them elected members of the Northern Ireland Assembly and nine independent members chosen from a range of organizations, including business, trade unions, community groups, voluntary organizations, and the legal profession. The chief constable of the PSNI is responsible to the Policing Board and not to the secretary of state. The Patten Report recommends that the function of the board should be to hold the Chief Constable and the Police Service publicly to account. There were also changes in management structures at a geographical level in order to allow for accountability mechanisms in relation to local communities. New Command Units are being established that correspond to local council areas, and it is intended that District Policing Partnership Boards will be established in each of these areas. These boards will be composed of both elected and independent members, and an important part of their task will be to present community concerns and priorities to the district commander. A senior police officer in Londonderry claimed that such boards were the only way forward to attain trust through inclusion. He reckoned that "they will be a pain in the butt for me but they will work. When people see a [non-conflict-related] strategy working as, for example, an anti-drugs initiative they will support it" (interview with PSNI officer, 2002).

Constantine (2001), the commissioner appointed to oversee the reform of policing, claimed that the total Patten Report recommendations would "stand or fall" on the success of the District Policing Partnership Boards. From another perspective an indication of the perceived potential of these boards is that, at the time of writing, some of their members are receiving death threats from extreme Republican elements.

The Office of the Police Ombudsman has now been established. A report from that office that was highly critical of police handling of the investigation of a terrorist bombing resulted in discord between the ombudsman and the chief constable. It may be that such friction will be an inescapable element of policing in transition.

It would seem that in Northern Ireland attempts are being made to achieve legal accountability (through the office of the ombudsman) and democratic accountability (through inter alia the District Police Partnership Boards).

HUMAN RIGHTS

No other profession working in the criminal justice system has the potential to infringe human rights as much as the police. Equally no other profession has the capacity to protect human rights in a democracy as much as police officers. (interview with PSNI officer, 2002)

Livingstone (2001) claims that, while police in Northern Ireland have had a very difficult job in the past thirty years, they have nevertheless infringed upon the human rights of others primarily in the areas of public order policing, conduct of search and arrest operations, and treatment of suspects in custody. Traditionally, human rights issues did not have high priority in the training and practices of the RUC. In fact, in 1999 the Patten Report revealed that only two out of seven hundred training sessions were given over to human rights. Recommendation 4 of the Patten Report proposes that

> All police officers and police civilians should be trained (and updated
> as required) in the fundamental principles and standards of human
> rights and the practical implications for policing. The human rights
> dimension should be integrated in to every module of police training
> and awareness of human rights issues and respect for human rights in
> the performance of duty should be an important element in the
> appraisal of individuals in the police service. (107)

The need for such training was exemplified during one human rights lecture for
Special Branch officers. In the context of a debate on the rights of the elderly, the
lecturer (a senior police officer) referred to them as "custard dribbling old fools"! It
is hardly surprising that the Northern Ireland Human Rights Commission had
serious concerns about the training given on the Human Rights Act (1998) and, in
particular, how it was received by some Special Branch officers. It was also recommended that the monitoring of human rights performance should be the responsibility of the Policing Board. All new officers will take a new oath, which expresses an explicit commitment to the upholding of human rights. Existing officers may
take the oath but, because they have already been attested, cannot be required to
do so. This has caused disquiet among some politicians and human rights activists
who have called for all officers to be required to take the oath. (It was argued by several Serbian police officers commenting on police reform that existing officers have
the most need to take, and be bound by, such an oath.) It is in this area of human
rights that the need for training in Northern Ireland is most acute. In this regard,
Crawshaw (1999) argues for the importance of making a distinction between
human rights "training" and "education." The former refers to the transmission of
skills and the latter to intellectual, moral, and social instruction.

TRAINING

The quality and ethos of a police service is determined largely by the training, education, and development its officers receive. As society changes, policing must
change to keep pace. The development of new techniques and equipment that can
aid good policing also creates complex problems in the areas of, for example, human
rights and the privacy of individuals. Throughout Europe operational police performance is coming under increased scrutiny, established practices are being questioned, and the body of legislation that informs policing is growing and changing.

The Commission on Policing for Northern Ireland consulted with police
and affiliated organizations in the United Kingdom, the United States, Canada,
Spain, and Holland. In the specific context of training, particular attention was
paid to the models of the Royal Canadian Mounted Police and the South African

Police Service. The resulting Patten Report made detailed recommendations concerning training for the Police Service of Northern Ireland. These include

- a detailed analysis and review of training strategy
- greater civilian input into training
- a reduction of time spent devoted to drill
- problem solving and partnership and human rights approaches should be central to recruit training
- community awareness should be integrated into all aspects of training and should include all the main religious and political traditions in Northern Ireland

A prime objective was to get the community involved at the training level and give them some understanding of the capabilities and limitations of the PSNI. As the PSNI training strategy document states: "If the concepts of openness, transparency and accountability in the police service are to mean anything, we believe that the community should be involved in shaping the mould which shapes the police service they receive. In other words, the community should have an important say in the shaping of training, education and development of the police officers who serve them" (2001, 4).

Training is currently presented under core themes such as human rights, equal opportunities and community and race relations, community policing, and professional standards and ethics. Notwithstanding all of this, the Committee on the Administration of Justice (1999) suggests that the current police training program needs to be thoroughly overhauled and argues that research in other jurisdictions highlights that anything less than a complete overhaul of initial and in-service training practices will fail.

It would seem that there is a qualitative difference between the training given to new recruits and the in-service training of existing officers. This will cause problems in the future. New recruits are likely to meet with some difficulties when they go out to their command units, where they will come into conflict with the old culture. One officer interviewed by the author described it as "the unstoppable meeting the immovable" and argued that little real change will come about in terms of police reform until a critical mass has been achieved that "tips the organization over."

INCLUSION

The concept of inclusion has become an integral part of approaches to good governance and human rights. In fact, it is often seen as sine qua non in this context. However, it can be a difficult (perhaps the most difficult) element to implement in the process of police reform. Arguably, those involved in the conflict should also be involved in the solution. In South Africa, for example, the new police force includes members who were previously liberation fighters. In Northern Ireland the IRA has shown little interest in joining the PSNI, and it is unlikely they would ever be accepted. However, Sinn Féin, their political representatives, have argued for a Catholic police force for Catholic communities. In these areas rough justice, in the form of punishment beatings and kneecappings, are commonplace. This idea of community policing is also a priority of the new police service. But it should be remembered that such initiatives have the potential to institutionalize difference. The strategy has been employed by the most repressive of regimes. We should be careful not to confuse community policing with policed communities.

SERBIA AND MONTENEGRO

On October 5, 2000, after a decade of sanctions, international isolation, NATO bombings, poverty, and dictatorship, in front of a massive crowd of disaffected Serbs, a demoralized police force surrendered to the overwhelming need for the political and economic reform of Serbia. In fact, so integral was the Serbian police to the regime that, arguably, the primary factor for the success of the popular movement to overthrow Slobodan Milosevic was its refusal, for the first time, to intervene on behalf of its political masters. Many police officers in Serbia refer to October 5, 2000, as the day that marked the new beginning for policing there.

Over the previous decade, in a complex and violent environment, the police had become the principal instrument of maintaining the government's power and curbing dissension in the Federal Republic of Yugoslavia. Monk (2001) argues that its collusion in upholding party political aims had turned it into a corrupt, unaccountable, and militant police organization largely mistrusted by the people of Serbia. As Babovic writes, "The police defended the regime against the citizens; the regime protected the police from legal responsibility" (2002, 67). By refusing to confront the protesters, the police effectively ended this understanding between it and the governing party.

This was a dramatic change for a policing institution with its roots in an authoritarian regime where the police had been organized as a people's militia, based on self-management concepts, to enforce the ideologies of the Communist Party. It has been described by Crampton (2002) as "an intricate and pervasive police system." Non-uniformed political police fulfilled an infiltrative role in Yugoslav society, while uniformed police officers were expected simply to be obedient to the party and to maintain a visible presence on the streets. This tradition

seems to have progressed beyond Tito's era into the 1980s. Even today police officers often comment on how little "policing" they actually performed under
Milosevic, adding that crime figures were absurdly low. When asked about their
duties, officers invariably mention security and public order duties.

As Yugoslavia began to feel the effects of serious economic decline and infla-
tion in the 1980s, low-level corruption crept into the culture of policing, as uniformed officers began to seek various ways to supplement the declining value of
their income. In the 1990s, while sanctions were being implemented upon
Serbia, corruption became so endemic that "policemen [were] almost constant-
ly offered compensation for not carrying out their duties" (Babovic 2002, 71). A
more insidious side effect of economic decline was the rise of nationalism and
the consequent outbreak of war as Yugoslavia violently split apart.

Power struggles between the Yugoslav Army (JNA) and Slobodan Milosevic
in the early 1990s gave him reason to have greater trust in the Ministry of
Internal Affairs than the military. Consequently, the power of the Serbian police
was slowly increased vis-à-vis the Federal Police and the army. This was achieved
by the gradual militarization of the police throughout the 1990s. The internal
structure of the police was reorganized in 1995 to reflect its military role. Police
officers were issued a revolver and an automatic machine gun, while uniform
police officers were issued mortars, bazookas, and other rocket guns (Babovic
2002). The Police Academy placed heavy emphasis on military training.
Moreover, Special Police Units of the State Security Service such as the paramilitary "Red Berets" (JSO) often supported and led key military operations. Glenny
(1999) cites the example of a police offensive launched in March 1998 on
Drenica, Kosovo, which led to the deaths of twenty-two Albanian fighters, triggered a flight of the civilian population, and directly contributed to the escalation of the conflict. At one stage it was estimated that, besides police assault
troops and secret police, over 5,000 Serb uniformed police officers were
deployed to Kosovo during the war, leaving a skeleton force to ensure public
order was maintained at home. One police officer in Belgrade claimed that over
three-quarters of his station served with him for two consecutive tours of duty
in Kosovo. U.S. intelligence estimates claim that a total of 20,000 officers under
the jurisdiction of the Serbian Ministry of Internal Affairs were at one stage
operating in Kosovo (Trivunovic 2003). That the Police Academy and the
Ministry of Internal Affairs Headquarters in Belgrade were bombed during the
NATO bombardment in 1999 is testimony to the extent, and political importance, of police involvement in Serbia's hostilities throughout the decade. The
International Criminal Tribunal for the Former Yugoslavia at The Hague has cat-
alogued extensive police involvement in war crimes perpetrated in Croatia,
Bosnia, and, in particular, Kosovo.

The blend of corruption, nationalism, and militarization in the Ministry of Internal Affairs produced an environment where underworld figures, criminals profiting from state-sanctioned organized crime, found solace in policing structures. It is believed that paramilitary "police" forces such as "Arkan's Tigers," "Seselj's White Eagles," and "Vucjak's Wolves," which operated in Kosovo, were co-opted into existing structures and provided with logistical and political support from the Serbian government. The existence of these special units, led by crime lords working under the authority of the Ministry of Internal Affairs, gives an indication of the extent to which Serbian society had become criminalized.

The reputation of the police diminished even further as the state authorities came to increasingly rely on them. Violent reactions to student demonstrations and to the ever-growing political opposition to the regime ensured that the majority of citizens associated the police with an undemocratic and repressive regime. Empirical surveys undertaken during the period indicated that the police were perceived as corrupt and that the public felt unwilling to report crime due to a general lack of trust (Kesetovic 2002).

DEFINING REFORM PRIORITIES

After October 2000 the Ministry of Internal Affairs, determined to prove its support for radical change, submitted a report to the Serbian National Assembly. This resulted in the assemblage of a "think tank": a group of Legal Experts (LEX), representatives of relevant nongovernmental organisations (NGOs), and members of the Danish Centre for Human Rights, who together created a "Mission and Vision Summary" document that would outline the reform strategy. This document included a list of thirteen "Values" to be incorporated in future reform. Among them it recommended the adoption of the European Code of Police Ethics and the UN Code of Conduct for Law Enforcement Officials. Furthermore, it spelled out its "Vision":

> Fundamental changes are yet to come ... based on [transforming the Ministry] into an organisation serving the citizens, that will perform the trusted duties strictly obeying the Constitution and the law. This implies respect and protection of human rights. ... The Ministry should be professional, de-politicized, efficient, subjected to democratic external control and oversight, polite, and have personal respect of the citizens. ... The organisation of the Ministry should be shared with community members. This will create a proactive approach, therefore involving members of the community. (Ministry of Internal Affairs 2000)

Much of this strategy derived from a special study of the policing in the Federal Republic of Yugoslavia commissioned by the Organisation for Security and Co-Operation in Europe (OSCE) in October 2001 to identify the most pertinent reform issues. It stated that "[after] a decade of isolation, chronic underinvestment in skills and resources and the use of the police for private political control . . . The police have become isolated from the community they serve . . . they are mistrusted by the public. . . . Policing has now to be effective against institutionalised levels of corruption and organised crime from within as well as from outside its ranks" (Monk 2001, 133). The report made 106 recommendations to modernize the Serbian police and bring it in line with international standards. Another influential report, undertaken on behalf of the Council of Europe (Slater 2001), focused on the need to inculcate a culture of human rights into the police culture and organization. It recommended a more community-oriented approach be taken so "that police establish co-operation with social bodies and civil society" (Slater 2001, 51). It advocated the recruitment of female police officers and recommended specific training be provided to all ranks of the organization in human rights. At a coordination meeting convened in Belgrade on December 17, 2001, the Serbian minister of internal affairs, Dusan Mihajlovic, named the OSCE as the leading coordinator of reform efforts and announced six priority areas of police reform:

- Police Education and Development: to rationalize and modernize police training in the Police College and the Police Academy
- Accountability and Internal Control: to establish an internal investigative unit, an external independent oversight body, and a parliamentary subcommittee
- Organized Crime: to enhance cooperation with other police forces, provide legislation and relevant training to combat organized crime, and upgrade existing resources in the Ministry of the Interior
- Forensics: to develop analysis capabilities and develop localized Crime Scene Management teams
- Border Policing: to improve the effectiveness of the Border Police Service on both "green" and "blue" borders through training, improved resources, and increased manpower
- Community Policing: to institute operational procedures and organizational structures conducive to community-oriented policing methods, thereby facilitating a partnership approach to local policing priorities

As leading coordinator of police reform, the OSCE utilizes policing experts in its Law Enforcement Department to support and assist the Ministry of Internal Affairs while maintaining governmental-level contacts through its Head of

Mission. The OSCE held a donors conference in June 2002 at which it was esti-
mated that 10.8 million Euro was required to further the immediate needs of
police reform in Serbia. Over 4.3 million Euro was pledged at the conference.
Pledges were made by, among others, the Institute for Democratic Control of
Armed Forces (DCAF), Denmark, Germany, the Netherlands, Norway, and the
United Kingdom (OSCE 2002).

MULTIETHNIC POLICING

Following Milosevic's fall in October 2000, a group calling itself the Liberation
Army of Presevo, Medvedja, and Bujanovac (UCPMB) and modelled after the
recently disbanded Kosovo Liberation Army (KLA) began to target Serb police
officers and civilians living in southern Serbia. This region had been included in
the agreement that ended the Kosovo war as a buffer zone inside Serbia proper
(drawn five kilometres from the Kosovo administrative line and the Macedonian
border) beyond which all Serb and Federal Republic of Yugoslavia (FRY) forces
had to withdraw. It is an underdeveloped region of Serbia, inhabited predominantly by an Albanian community legitimately aggrieved by its mistreatment
during the Milosevic regime. As had occurred in Kosovo, the region suffered
from economic neglect and heavy-handed Serbian security measures.
Unemployment was over 60 percent and local industry was in chronic decline.
In 1991 the practice of joint Serb-Albanian police patrols had been dispensed
with and replaced by Serb police and gendarmerie.

Despite the fact that, by October 2000, the Serbian police had relaxed its
security grip of the region, the UCPMB still sought autonomy from Belgrade and
wanted to unite the region with Kosovo. The Serb army, in turn, wanted to enter
the buffer zone, which was being utilized by the guerrillas to launch attacks. A
peace plan was devised by Nebojsa Covic, which aimed at satisfying the demands
of moderate Albanians. The plan was based on confidence-building measures
among ethnic communities in the region (Covic 2001). Albanians would be
integrated into the institutions of the Republic of Serbia, all inhabitants would
be disarmed, and the region would be targeted for economic revival. A pivotal
aspect of the plan was the creation of a multiethnic police service, comprising
proportionate numbers of officers from the Albanian and Serb communities.

Although initially rejected by the UCPMB, the Covic Plan was endorsed by
the international community, and in April 2001 the OSCE agreed to coordinate
the recruitment and training of the multiethnic police. The primary points of
contention that emerged during negotiations included the educational background of the candidates; the level of involvement of international trainers;

whether to use the existing ministry curriculum or devise a fresh one; the recruitment of UCPMB members to the force; and the related concern that Albanian candidates might be arrested during the application process. After extensive negotiations between leaders of the Albanian community, the international community, and Serb delegates, agreement was reached in these matters in the spirit of reconciliation and dialogue.

An initial five-day "refresher" course, followed by a five-week course, was presented to twenty-five Serbian and Albanian serving officers. These officers began joint patrols in the region on May 28, 2001. Both national and international staff taught at the college. New recruits received twelve-week courses based around a new curriculum that aimed to inculcate the values of human rights and community-oriented policing, while offering training in the use of defensive tactics and firearms. Issues arose concerning the rejection of certain candidates for "special reasons." It was claimed that some candidates had been rejected because their relatives had criminal records, although UCPMB members without "criminal or terrorist records" were eligible. The Albanian representatives felt that this was discriminatory. As a compromise the ministry agreed to review certain cases. According to a source involved in the process, Albanian community leaders were deeply involved in the selection process. He pointed out that although this transferred ownership of the project to the community, it was questionable whether all of these candidates would necessarily make potentially good police officers. The reality is that more than half of the Kosovo police force were formerly in the Kosovo Liberation Army.

Significantly, twenty-eight female police officers attended and graduated from the course. These were the first female patrolling officers in Serbia. Following the intensive twelve-week class-based course, recruits were required to participate in fifteen weeks of "on-the-job training," or field training, where each trainee worked alongside an experienced officer. Additionally, there was a twenty-four-week probation period.

IMPLEMENTING POLICE REFORM

The six priority reform areas identified in December 2001 are long-term projects that are currently at early stages of development. Ministry Working Groups have been set up to develop each area in cooperation with the OSCE, whose familiarity with international models is being utilized to develop implementation plans. Some progress has been made. At a meeting in Vrnjacka Banja, in central Serbia, on April 19, 2002, the minister stated that new laws on internal affairs, security services, the opening of secret police files, and the fight against organized crime are strategic goals; the aim is to be the best according to European standards.

In 2002 the Interpol office in Belgrade was re-established and work got underway on the process of harmonizing existing legislation with a recently passed law on Special Competencies on the Suppression of the Organised Crimes and Corruption. Also, it is anticipated that special bodies will be developed within the current administration of the justice system, which includes the establishment of a Special Prosecutors Office, Police Unit, and Court and Detention Centre. In order to improve internal control, an Inspector General's Office has been opened within the Ministry of Internal Affairs.

A process of training border police has commenced with concomitant upgrading of border posts and the establishment of mobile immigration/border police teams. Laws are also being prepared to decentralize police and to ensure greater local accountability. It is proposed that the local authorities will select their own chief of police for a municipality, with the approval of the minister, and that he or she will become a member of the municipal executive authority, formalizing a direct link between police and local government. The objective is to facilitate more community-oriented policing strategies.

Just as in Northern Ireland, the head of the Working Group for Community Policing stated in an interview that there "is no alternative to community policing." The ministry initiated a crime prevention scheme in November 2001 and deployed police officers to over 250 schools throughout the country to monitor and prevent crime on playgrounds. This program has boasted impressive results, with drug abuse down by 95 percent in participating schools. Parents have expressed satisfaction for the work of the "school policeman." Additionally, community policing projects have commenced at five pilot municipalities. It is anticipated that the results of these projects will enable the ministry to develop a plan to be used throughout the country. As an evaluation tool and a guide for both police and the public, a public perception survey has been undertaken, and its results will assist police and the public in deciding on policing priorities. Consultation meetings between police, representatives of civil society, local opinion leaders, and local government were held in December 2002. The Roma community, which has suffered especially discriminatory policing practices, is being encouraged to participate.

In-service training has been running since September 2002 in an attempt to encourage police officers to become more community and service orientated. By December 2002, 2,500 men and women had attended the Modern Policing Course, which is based on the concepts of democratic policing and human rights in a pluralistic environment. It is intended that the Serbian Ministry of the Interior will take over training from international trainers. As well as training, more visible examples of change have been made. For example, new uniforms have been provided and all police officers now wear a name tag in Cyrillic script. (Unlike Northern Ireland, these symbolic changes have received a general welcome from the public.) The most dramatic change in policing in Serbia is the presence of 346 newly graduated female police officers, the first-ever female officers to patrol the streets of Belgrade and other major cities.

The progress made so far by Serbian authorities would seem to be related in no small way to the country's application for entry to the European Union, made in 2004. "Police reform is part of the overall reform process in Serbia which is aimed at making sure the country is ready for European integration by 2004" (Mihajlovic 2002, 73). The law enforcement department at the OSCE testifies to considerable levels of commitment from ministry officials. While the multiethnic police force was a key stability mechanism to end the conflict in southern Serbia, the new uniform changes and the presence of female officers have certainly made a positive difference. Maybe, however, it is the small things that have the most significant effects. As one resident from Kragujevac put it, "the women police officers all smile while they write you your fines. To me it's a positive step."

It is, however, difficult to gauge the long-term success of reform. It is notable that although Serbs, in general, discern a difference in the police since October 5, 2000, they also express concerns that reform will not be deep enough and that the structural changes necessary to democratize policing will not be made. They point to the fact that the leadership of the ministry has not altered, although a number of senior personnel changes were made in January 2003. These changes were undertaken in order to strengthen the influence of Serbian Prime Minister Zoran Djindjic's Democratic Party (DS) in the security system and purge it of the remnants of the Milosevic regime.

These changes also saw a new minister of interior appointed, Nenad Milic. His primary goal will be to root out corruption in the force. Daily newspapers regularly report connections between police and organized crime that contribute to the public's distrust of police. At another level, there does not exist a police union for police officers in Serbia. A resultant danger may be that reform efforts are being dictated in a top-down manner. One senior official, commenting on resistance in some police organizations emanating from unions, claimed that "we don't have that problem here; they do what we tell them. They have no choice."

Moreover, the effectiveness of training courses has yet to be proven. Although the Modern Policing Course is extremely well evaluated by participating officers, some individual police officers are unhappy with the content, saying it was far too basic and that it will probably not affect police behavior. More seriously, problems have surfaced with the multiethnic police in southern Serbia. Citizens in the region perceive the force as something separate from the "ordinary" police. They do not regard the officers as "real police officers." This is primarily because multiethnic police officers have not been integrated into the policing structure and have been kept as a separate entity. Additionally, the original proposal that all police in the region would be multiethnic and be appropriately trained was not fully implemented. The region is still very heavily policed by both gendarmerie, "ordinary" police and multiethnic police. The issue of Kosovo's final status is still debated, and there has been increased tension, with multiethnic officers coming under attack.

CONCLUSION

While caution is essential when attempting to draw general conclusions from case study data, there do nonetheless seem to be common aspects regarding police reform emanating from the selected sites. Underlying almost all of the concerns expressed and observed therein was the overarching concept of trust. At the macro level Darby (2001) has argued that the initial and major concern of governments is to test the seriousness of militants before considering reducing the security apparatus. He claims that the confidence- and trust-building measures demanded by ex-militants such as early release of prisoners, police reform, etc., are equally predictable. On the ground what is essential is the development of trust within the police force and trust of the police by the public that the embryonic force is designed to serve. The latter is likely to be enhanced through a cooperative public/police response to crime. In early post-accord years this might only be possible in the treatment of nonpolitical crime such as drug dealing, smuggling, burglary, etc. These are the very types of crime that seem to increase after conflicts cease. Paradoxically, such crime and the treatment of it may cement a hitherto unknown understanding and acceptance of reforming police forces. However, in Northern Ireland and elsewhere, those most involved in crime are those who previously were active in the conflict. The emerging police force, therefore, will now be tackling criminals who in the past may have acted as protectors of, and were protected by, the communities of which they form part. There is likely to be a strong residual community identity with these individuals.

In addition, the steps necessary to restore some form of normality (searches, curfews, check points, etc.) are exactly those most likely to engender antagonism. There is a danger, therefore, that attempts to maintain law and order may be seen by the public as simply a new kind of control. Nowhere is this more evident than in post-conflict Iraq. The forces there seem to have gravely underestimated this aspect of reform. What is vital here is a sense of ownership of institutions that are accessible and transparent structures to which the police are accountable. In Northern Ireland such accountability is provided through the

Police Board and the Office of Police Ombudsman; in Serbia it would seem that there is less certainty that such structural changes aimed at increased accountability will take place. Perhaps accountability is, more than any other aspect in a reform process, dependant on a strong government commitment to the concept.

Community policing is often presented as an essential part of the process of changing the role of the police from a control function to a service-orientated approach. Officers in both Serbia and Northern Ireland emphasized the importance of the strategy. However, good governance in general, and community policing in particular, demands inclusion, and this concept has inherent problems. At the level of induction, these problems revolved around the introduction of a 50:50 balance of Catholic and Protestant applicants to the Police Service of Northern Ireland. In Serbia the problems were of an ethnic nature between Serbs, Albanians, and Roma. At another level, it is difficult for reformers to totally accept the adage that since paramilitaries were part of the problem, they should also be part of the solution. This is especially germane in the appointment to a police force of those who were "branded" as murderers in the past. A final caveat might be appropriate here. With regard to the District Command Units in Northern Ireland and the institution of operational procedures and organizational structures conducive to community-oriented policing in Serbia (both designed to decentralize policing and foster local ownership of the reform process), there may be a danger that the greater the attempts to match policing to particular communities, the greater may be the danger of actually institutionalizing difference.

The nature of post-appointment training is also likely to be of the utmost importance in terms of the effectiveness and acceptance of a reforming police service. There seemed to be, however, a fair amount of skepticism among officers concerning the ability of training to change the culture of policing. One station commander claimed that senior officers loyal to Milosevic after October 2000 "simply learned to swim with the new current." A senior officer in Northern Ireland stated that new recruits were experiencing something like "the unstoppable meeting the immovable" as the enthusiasm of the young encountered the intransigence of those who were long established. In the context of general post-conflict reform, Dunn claims that "the power or the potential of internal [influences] to contribute to the social and psychological atmosphere that might allow conflict to be reduced is rarely examined" (1995, 5).

It is likely that internal conflicts and differences will continue to exist during the process of post-conflict police reform. There are two lessons here. In the first place, equal attention should be given to in-service and pre-service training. In post-conflict situations this is not always the case. Secondly, it would seem to be misguided (and probably counterproductive) to expect that meaningful change in policing will be observed within developing police forces until a critical mass is reached when "post-conflict" recruits have reached the stage of having at least as much influence in decision making as the "old guard." What is abundantly clear is that, notwithstanding training and structural innovation, little will be achieved in terms of post-accord police reform without concomitant attitudinal and cultural change. This raises what is possibly the most crucial dilemma for those involved in such reform. On the one hand, police reform must be an essential early priority, but equally, the success of such reform will depend on the rather longer-term issues such as the creation of legitimate government and a context in which trust can be built.

In fact, the concept of trust is of overarching importance in the process of police reform. Officers who may be undergoing such reform, especially if it is enforced, are likely to be fearful of losing their hitherto unquestioned position. They will therefore often prove to be, at best, reluctant reformers. The public, on the other hand, may have become accustomed to fearing the police force or at least distrusting them. These perceptions are unlikely to change overnight. What is essential, therefore, to the process of police reform is that at least as much attention be given to winning hearts and minds as to any structural innovations.

With regard to reconciliation processes in general, Lederach (2002) cautions against being distracted into thinking that a single aspect is the entire process. He argues for a "thick approach" where it is essential to focus on the context, which involves people, place, history, and culture. Nowhere is this more apposite than in the context of police reform. It applies equally to police forces and to the communities that they are attempting to serve. It will demand both long-term and holistic approaches to police reform. Piecemeal reform is likely to be no reform at all.

Finally, it is important to stress that post-conflict police reform is not an end in itself but rather an essential part of a reconciliation process. Too often in the past, post-accord reform has foundered as a result of frustrated expectations arising from a lack of appreciation of this fact.

ROGER MAC GINTY

Post-Accord Crime

Media accounts of societies emerging from protracted ethnonational conflicts commonly paint a negative picture. Whether from Bosnia, South Africa, or Lebanon, the narrative is often one of simmering tensions at the local level left unresolved by macrolevel political settlements, unfulfilled public expectations, poverty, and crime. Reports on crime often have a shrill, alarmist quality, reinforcing the idea that peace has been somehow squandered. Newspaper headlines help make the point: "Sex, Drugs and Illegal Migrants: Sarajevo's Export Trade to Britain," or, from South Africa, "Police Chief 'Ran Drugs Extortion Racket.'"[1]

No obvious single theoretical lens helps explain the seemingly "counterintuitive phenomenon" (Call 1999, 1) in which the postwar peace is more violent than the war it succeeds. A number of concepts offer insights, however. Human security is useful in positing commentary on security firmly within a broader framework of development and introduces the neglected notion of human dignity.[2] Literature on transnational organized crime is useful in identifying how globalization has facilitated the development of criminal networks with an extensive geographical reach and the deftness of these organizations in advantageously aligning themselves with an evolving global economy.[3] Although the recipient of significant media and political attention, transnational organized crime (TOC) remains an unsatisfactory frame of reference, not least because crime in the aftermath of violent political conflict need not necessarily be transnational or organized.[4]

Insights are offered by transition studies, particularly in providing accounts of how post-communist and post-authoritarian states have sought to manage economic and political liberalization. Many parallels exist between the crime surges experienced in post–peace accord and transition societies (see Moran 2001; Shaw 2002). Critical and legal reformism criminology is also useful, particularly in investigating the impact of democratic transitions and communitarian strategies on fledgling criminal justice systems (Van Zyle Smit 1999). It is the peculiar heritage of ethnonational conflicts, however, and the nature of contemporary peace processes, that demand a specialized account of post-accord crime. For this reason, the nature of ethnonational conflict is regarded as the most appropriate lens for this study. Particularly important to the explanation of post-accord crime is the blurring of the civil and military spheres in ethnonational conflict and the persistence of this blurring in the post-accord period. Postwar crime is neither novel nor restricted to the aftermath of violent ethnonational conflict, but since these conflicts have dominated the post–Cold War period, they are the focus of the current work.[5] In short, post–peace accord crime is highly context dependent.

The chapter begins by outlining some of the difficulties associated with reaching a definition of "post–peace accord crime." It then suggests that the peculiar nature of ethnonational conflicts will have a significant influence on post-accord crime. A chief "peculiarity" of ethnonational conflict is the blurring of the distinction between the military and civilian spheres and the extent to which the civil-military overlap can extend into the post-accord period and facilitate crime. The chapter also comments on the problems of gauging the incidence of post-accord crime and the difficulties of classification. The chapter then moves on to illustrate features of post-accord societies that may make them more susceptible to crime.

Although crime often has objective attributes, the dynamics and qualities associated with ethnonational conflicts provide crime with an additional subjective dimension. This subjective dimension will largely be constructed according to how groups interpret their position in the post-conflict environment: is the group winning/losing or secure/insecure? Post–peace accord crime has the potential to become a lens through which parties to a conflict interpret their position in the process of coming out of that conflict. The scale, motivation, source, and targeting of crime will all be scrutinized as indicators of the state of the peace. In sum, the perception of crime deserves as much attention as crime itself.

Defining Post–Peace Accord Crime

Perhaps the most significant issue associated with any examination of post-accord conventional crime is one of definition. The term "post-accord" is chosen in preference to "post-conflict" in recognition that complex ethnonational conflicts rarely end in a definitive manner. While violence, or a certain level of violence, may cease or become more manageable, the latent bases of the conflict often persist. A ceasefire or formal peace accord brings no guarantee of an end to violence by militants, and both may prompt deliberate attempts by some antagonists to derail peace efforts.[6] Peace processes can become protracted and provide antagonists with further sites of competition, again making a definitive conflict endpoint difficult to identify.[7] For the purposes of this chapter, "post-accord" is taken as the period after the agreement and ratification of a major peace accord involving the main actors in a conflict, including the governing party.

A further problem of definition relates to the term "crime." The term is general, conceivably encompassing a vast range of activity. For the purposes of this chapter, a broad definition of crime is maintained: violent and nonviolent activity perpetrated by individuals and groups (including the state) and transgressing a legal code. The main focus of this chapter is on violent crime. In any context, the term "crime" is a label—immediately pejorative and condemnatory, and extending beyond objective categorizations of transgressions against the law. In societies marked by protracted conflict, the definition of what constitutes a crime and who has criminal liability can be informed by ethnic cleavages. Some groups may hold privileged positions in the state and may possess "naming power," or the ability to brand certain types of behavior as deviant and other types as acceptable. Similarly, the behavior of certain groups in ethnically contested territories will be subject to judgment on deviance or acceptability according to an ethnic lens. Given that ethnic perceptions are essentially malleable and capable of both entrenchment and radicalization, they present peculiar problems for conceptualizations of crime, law, order, and justice.

The term "crime" also presupposes an authority with both the legitimacy and the capability to enforce law, a situation not always prevailing in a post-accord situation. While a peace settlement may make provision for a new legal code, reform of the judiciary, and the recruitment, training, and reorganization of a law enforcement force, this may not necessarily translate into public acceptance of the law. In conflicts with an ethnonational dimension, certain groups may be resistant to law reform and regard a new legal code as discriminatory. This problem of "what constitutes a crime" may be further compounded by uncertainty arising from a transitional period during which the new legal code is introduced and the criminal justice sector restructured.

The Blurring of the Military-Civilian Spheres in Ethnonational Conflicts

Perhaps the thorniest definitional problem relates to the issue of what constitutes "conventional" crime. Put simply, in the context of an ethnonational conflict there is no clear dividing line between nonpolitical or pure criminal activity within a civilian sphere and military activity by clearly defined combatants. This is largely due to the peculiar nature of ethnonational conflict and the routine crossover of military and civilian activity. The areas of overlap between the military and civilian spheres will include military activity that can be termed "criminal" and that may lie within the domain of civilian crime.[8] The significance of these areas of overlap for any account of post-accord crime arises from the persistence of ethnonational conflict, which often continues beyond any formal peace accord. The patterns of overlap between the military and civilian spheres during conflict often survive the ending of the violent phase of the conflict and can be instructive of post-accord patterns of crime and violence. Without empirical data it is impossible to assert that the types of conflict and civil-military overlap found during conflict are predictive of post-accord crime and violence. But it does not stretch common sense too far to suggest that, depending on context, patterns of violence may persist into the post-accord phase. As will be explained in more detail below, societies with violent conflicts that ordinarily include rape, kidnap, and theft as component parts of a military campaign will, at a minimum, contain individuals skilled in crime and communities partially complicit in these activities.

Five key areas of military-civilian overlap are identified: personnel, the modus operandi of violent actors, the legal code employed during the conflict, the geographical sites of the conflict, and the causes of the conflict. The first of these factors, personnel, relates to both victims and perpetrators in ethnonational conflicts, who often manage to simultaneously occupy the civilian and military spheres. A defining feature of many conflicts has been the "civilianized" nature of combatants. Apart from formal military forces, ethnonational conflicts have seen the deployment of militarized police, part-time militias, shady "third forces," paramilitaries, mercenaries, organic guerilla forces, and civilian mobs. Many of these groups simultaneously inhabit both the civilian and military spheres. The Sri Lankan government, for example, has raised a militia "homeguard," mainly made up of Sinhalese farmers in "cleared areas," to defend against attacks by Tamil militants. Tending their crops while armed, they are at once potential victims and antagonists. Similarly, some Kosovan farmers cleared from their homes by Serb militias in 1999 may also have been members of the Kosovo Liberation Army, again simultaneously inhabiting both civilian and military positions in society.

The structural and embedded nature of intergroup perceptions during ethnonational conflicts also demonstrate the conflation of the military and civilian categories. Antagonists are often objectified and demonized, with whole peoples regarded as an undifferentiated mass. Thus, in Rwanda many extreme Hutus regarded Tutsis simply as Tutsis regardless of age, sex, profession, or political affiliation. This denial of intragroup differences can have profound consequences for interpretations of crime during a conflict. The perceptual framework that allows a group of people to be labeled as "the enemy" and justified as a legitimate target will probably exclude the possibility that the same group could be considered as potential victims of crime. Similarly, according to this viewpoint, the demonized group will not be worthy of protection by law.

A second area of overlap between the civilian and military spheres in situations of ethnonational conflict relates to the modus operandi of organized militant groups. This overlap is particularly prominent in relation to criminal activity. Take, for example, the actions involved in ethnic cleansing. Intimidation, criminal damage, and theft are not the mainstays of conventional military-on-military violence.[9] Instead, they sit more comfortably in the milieu of civilian crime. The context of violent ethnonational conflict (the presence of organized groups, linkages to political causes, a permissive environment for group-on-group violence) means that activity ordinarily deemed "criminal" can assume a place in a military campaign. In the former Yugoslavia, it was extremely common for the expulsion of a community to be followed by the theft of their property, whether agricultural equipment or business premises.[10] Furthermore, crime in the form of theft, extortion, or smuggling is a common method of financing conflict. Mittelman and Johnston (1999, 15) note how religious and ethnic cleavages in conflict societies can seamlessly meld with arms and drugs trafficking. Even a single incident can illustrate the difficulty of distinguishing between the civilian and military spheres: the proceeds from an armed robbery may be split between the pockets of the perpetrators and the coffers of the politico-military organization to which they are affiliated.

The legal code in a conflict area provides a third area of overlap between the military and civilian spheres. A legal system may be specifically designed or modified to apply to a conflict situation. For example, the level of proof required for a conviction for certain acts may be lowered. The same legal system, and the same law enforcement officers, however, will usually be expected to deal with nonpolitical offenses. The result may be a politicization of the entire legal system and its incorporation into the war effort. Indeed, many states have adopted a deliberate policy of "criminalization" toward ethnonational dissent within their own borders. While the aim may be to deny dissenters political legitimacy by suppressing any violence through the civil code and "police action," the result may be the compromising of civil law. This politicization of the law during conflict can have significant after effects in a post-accord period.

Another area of overlap between the military and civilian spheres that will have a bearing on post–peace accord crime relates to the geographical sites of conflict. Ethnonational disputes are often marked by the proximity of combatants and identifiable ethnic groups (Darby 1995, 2). They share space or live in close proximity, and the physical "battlefield" takes the form of towns, villages, workplaces, and public space. Again, the distinction between the civilian and military spheres is blurred. In the post-accord phase, mixed settlement patterns may persist, with minorities living among (formerly) hostile majority communities. As a result, some crime is likely to take a cross-community form and be open to interpretation as a political act.

A final area of crossover between the military and civilian spheres in situations of ethnonational conflicts lies in the causes of conflict. A major discussion of the causes of conflict is beyond the scope of the current chapter. Ideology, ethnicity, biology, insecurity, symbolism, grievances, and economics have all been promoted—singly or in combinations—as possible causes of conflict and violence (see Azar 1990, 7–12; Brown et al. 1997, 3–25; Kaufman 2001, 1–13). Explanations vary according to the level of analysis, with individuals, communities, and states all displaying different motivations and adopting different methods of decision making. Despite the complexity, one possible cause and maintainer of violence is worth considering because of the current focus on crime: economic advantage. The "greed thesis" on conflict causation prioritizes economic predation above other explanations, including religious or ethnic polarization, and has the capacity to be a motivating factor for both individuals and larger groups. Collier (2000) notes that economic predation can be a major factor in motivating rebellion, particularly in cases where high-value, portable resources such as diamonds are concerned. Similarly, De Soysa (2002, 413) regards the availability of natural resources to be "a potent predictor of conflict." It is worth noting that the presence of spoils ("valuable, easily tradeable commodities") is one of the key factors in thwarting the implementation of peace accords (Stedman, Rothchild, and Cousens 2002, 3). Although the greed thesis often makes claims based on unreliable data sets and imprecise conceptualizations, the focus on predatory accumulation as a cause and sustaining factor behind conflict is worthwhile. Moreover, the underlying motiva-tion—personal gain—is likely to persist into the post-accord period. Put simply, blood diamonds do not lose their value because elites sign a peace accord.

The significance of the above-mentioned points of crossover (personnel, modus operandi, legal system, geography, and conflict causes) is that they may extend into the post-accord period. Post-accord crime may resemble violence during the conflict and may even be regarded as an extension of the conflict itself, despite the agreement of a peace accord between political leaders. The key to this is perception.[11] Crime is rarely an objective fact; instead, it depends on definition and interpretation. In post–peace accord situations, actors at all levels may be hypersensitive to perceived slights, targeting, and attacks. Political lead-ers may be ready to interpret attacks on the individual as attacks on the commu-nity and seek political explanations of "criminal" activity. The incidence of crime against a certain community, and the willingness of the authorities to deal with it, may be taken as a litmus test of the inclusion of that community within a post-accord political dispensation. To complicate matters, victims and perpetra-tors in deeply divided societies are capable of holding radically different interpre-tations of the same incident. The perpetrator of a street mugging may regard the incident as a simple economic action; for the victim, however, the act may be much more. Indeed, the economic motive may be merely incidental to more sig-nificant political factors: the attacker was from a different ethnic group, used more violence than was necessary, or was making a statement about the control of territory or the subordination of one group by another.

THE INCIDENCE AND CLASSIFICATION OF POST-ACCORD CRIME

Post-accord crime is not endemic, nor does a peace accord automatically herald a crime surge. Namibia, for example, has largely escaped South Africa's crime lev-els. There is a danger of an "over-homogenised imagery" in which societies com-ing out of conflict are equated with lawlessness and criminality (Edwards and Gill 2002, 247). Instead, a more carefully nuanced approach is required in which the methods and motivations for calculating the incidence of post-accord crime are treated with caution. In the first place, it is impossible to delineate with pre-cision between prior existing wartime criminal trends and post-accord crime. The specifically "post-accord" elements of post-accord crime may be so embed-ded in contextual factors that they are impossible to identify. During a violent conflict and in the immediate post-accord period, the recording and reporting mechanisms for crime statistics are likely to be distorted. In periods of political violence, police forces may direct relatively few resources to conventional crime. Car theft may seem inconsequential when set within a context of car bombings. Less than meticulous recording of civil crime during a violent conflict may mean that post-accord crime statistics start from a low base, and recorded year-by-year increases may seem particularly high in the initial post-accord period.

Furthermore, citizens may have greater confidence in reporting crime to the police in a post-accord environment. They may be convinced that the police will take conventional crime seriously. A reassertion of civil law, and a return to normality for business, may even mean that it is worthwhile to report crime to the authorities for insurance or civil suit purposes. In the context of a deeply divided society, a reorganization of the police force may make the police more acceptable and encourage groups who may have been alienated from the police to report crime. Rather than a politicized force of oppression, a post–peace accord police force may come to be regarded as a functional agency for law enforcement. Increasing levels of reported crime may indicate increasing confidence in the police rather than increasing crime rates per se.

Another methodological consideration relates to the need to place post-accord crime trends in the context of global and regional crime trends. It may be that crime is increasing in the region, but an emphasis on the post-accord society encourages the regional context to be overlooked. The global context of the "war on terror" has also cast its shadow on discourses on crime in post-accord societies. A sprawling conceptual category of activity related to "terrorism" has developed to encompass and criminalize a range of activities that had previously been discussed using other discourses of insurgency, the informal state, and ethnonational conflict. Commentary on post-accord crime and transnational crime has been sucked into an often shrill vortex of discussion on "terrorism" and has been distorted in the process.

Post-accord crime may also be more visible simply because the backdrop of political violence has declined. Police forces and news organizations, used to focusing on political violence, may be free to turn their attention to criminal activities. Changing patterns of criminal behavior may contribute to the increased visibility of crime. In South Africa, for example, much crime has "migrated" from the black townships to the (mainly) white suburbs, becoming more visible in the process. Some sectors may even be tempted to inflate the threat from crime. Reform and reorganization of law enforcement agencies, a key part of many peace accords, may involve a severe downsizing of forces that became enlarged during periods of political violence. Two obvious arguments present themselves as a way of staving off savage budget cuts and job losses. The first is that the threat of political violence remains despite a peace accord. The second is that a new threat is emerging: crime. According to this argument, the crime that is emerging is of a magnitude and type somehow different from crime found in other societies. It is as though post-accord crime is imbued with special qualities.

Another sector that may be tempted to exaggerate reports of post-accord crime are those opposed to the peace accord. According to this view, rising crime is yet another peace deficit. Attempts may be made to associate political enemies with crime as a way of undermining their legitimacy. For example, in Northern Ireland claims and counter-claims have been traded on the metamorphosis of politically motivated militant organizations into criminal organizations. By extension, the argument is made that the political cousins of these militant/criminal organizations have a cynical attitude toward the peace accord, and, therefore, they should be sanctioned.

Complicating methodological matters is the accompaniment of a post-accord crime surge with an exaggerated perception of a crime surge. Fear of crime may exceed the actual possibility of becoming a victim of crime. The fear of crime may also become suffused with a mix of other perceptual factors linked with calculations of the individual's or group's perceived position in the post-accord environment. Community discourses of disillusionment with the post-accord settlement are particularly vulnerable to distortion by single incidents, often cruelly violent. In the public imagination the exception can become the rule, fueling pessimism and disillusionment with the wider post-accord dispensation.

Any discussion of the incidence of post-accord crime needs to pay attention to the classification of crime. Clearly "crime" does not constitute an undifferentiated category, but the classification of crime may be particularly sensitive in a deeply divided society. Again we face the problem of the blurring of categories. Some crimes may be judged "para-political" in that they straddle the criminal and political spheres. In a conflict area, where the dividing line is drawn often depends on where one stands. At a minimum, it seems important to attempt to distinguish between key types of crime and to assess their impact on the post-accord peace. Certain types of crime and violence (for example, attacks by spoiler groups) may be a direct challenge to the peace process or post-accord political dispensation. The labeling of such attacks as "crime" marks a deliberate statement by those committed to the accord that the situation has moved on and political violence lacks legitimacy.

Intergroup crime is also worthy of distinct classification. In many deeply divided societies, most crime is intragroup, with residential segregation providing a significant restraint on crime between groups. Intergroup crime may indicate a continuation of the conflict between ethnic groups. Again, perception is crucial. Violent attacks on white farmers in South Africa have attracted significant attention, not least because of controversy over the complex motivations behind such attacks. Are they robbery, racist, or both? The South African government has equivocated in attaching a racist motivation to these attacks, yet it seems important that police-reporting mechanisms have a capacity to record intergroup crime as a separate category.

Public and mob violence is also worthy of classification in that it can constitute a threat to the legitimacy of the new political dispensation. Guatemala, for instance, has witnessed a number of lynchings in its post-accord period.[12] There is a fine line between targeted and localized vigilante activities and mob rule and riots with a political motive. It is worth noting that vigilante violence can receive tacit support from the law enforcement branch of government, again undermining the claim of government to due process and a monopoly on violence.[13] Less public crime is also important, although it is difficult to gauge the impact it may have on the wider political environment. Levels of sexual and domestic violence in South Africa have reached alarming levels,[14] yet it is difficult to assert that this constitutes a threat to the political system. It does undermine the quality of peace, however, a point that will be revisited in the conclusion.

Another problem associated with the classification of post-accord crime is identifying an appropriate moment at which to end the timeline. Crime will adopt its own dynamics, evolving to suit the conditions in the post-accord environment. With time, criminal networks that were once exclusively the preserve of former combatants may change in profile, admitting those from a generation who were not directly involved in the conflict. Another complication with timing is that a post-accord increase in crime may be delayed, with post-accord euphoria creating a "period of grace" of high public expectation and commitments to the civic pluralism contained in a peace deal. Public disillusion, as a promised peace dividend fails to materialize, may play a key role in facilitating an increase in crime.

FACTORS CONTRIBUTING TO
POST-ACCORD CRIME

Having cautioned against an unquestioning acceptance of reports of rising post-accord crime, it is worth examining the factors that might contribute to any increase in post-accord crime. The causes of crime are the subject of intense debate, even in societies without a recent history of violent conflict. In post-accord societies, however, the history of conflict can create an environment conducive to crime. Six environmental factors contributing to post-accord crime are identified: state weakness, a culture permissive to crime, the presence—in large numbers—of former combatants and military weapons, the nature and scale of development aid, and uneven economic development. The link between these factors and crime is not automatic, although each has the capacity to significantly enhance an environment conducive to crime.

Under certain circumstances, conflict strengthens the state; for example, it may provide a rationale for the mobilization of resources and the quashing of dissent. In many cases, however, conflict weakens the state. In fact, the state may be the object of the conflict, with secessionists attempting to break from the state or wrest greater autonomy from the center. Short of defeat and extinction, a state's pursuit of conflict can result in the erosion of internal and external legitimacy, divisions between elites, and an exhaustion of financial resources. These factors can continue into the post-accord period, helping to create an environment permissible for crime. Crucial here is the state's weak capability: porous borders, inadequate criminal justice systems, poor financial oversight of government activities, and corruption all provide opportunities for post-accord crime. Regional clusters of ethnonational conflicts (for example, the Balkans or the Horn of Africa) may mean a concentration of weak states and thus extensive geographical areas conducive to crime.

A transition or peace process may be marked by a vacuum of legitimate government whereby all parties recognize that the government, and its institutions such as the police force, will be subject to reform. In both Northern Ireland and South Africa, it was accepted during political negotiations that major police reform would form a key part of any accord. As a result, the authority of the police force is eroded during the crucial transitional period.

Weak states may also be marked by the presence of centers of power other than the state. These rivals to the state may include sections of the armed forces, former combatants, strong political parties, or business organizations, all of whom may engage in crime with the knowledge that the state has limited powers of censure. Economic motivations may be particularly prominent in explaining the persistence of rivals to the state. For warlords, corrupt military officials, and multinational corporations, the state may only serve a purpose if it protects their interests. If the state is incapable of doing so then they will find their own mechanisms—outside of the law—to protect their extraction of power and wealth. For many, the state may not be the obvious provider of security. A lengthy conflict may have habituated certain groups or localities so completely with the notion of state incapacitation that nonstate bodies such as vigilantes will be a more obvious "policeman."

Linked to state weakness is a culture of conflict and violence that may extend into the post-accord period. While difficult to measure, it is reasonable to suggest that a protracted and violent ethnonational conflict will shape norms of behavior regarding obedience to the law and expectancy of apprehension for crimes. Although an elite-level peace accord may be reached, it is unlikely to prompt an immediate change in behavior at the local level, particularly if an environment of permissiveness is entrenched.[15] In a deeply divided society, the permissive environment in relation to crime may reflect ethnic cleavages and may persist in a post-accord era. For example, the security situation in some geographical areas during a conflict may have resulted in intermittent policing, or even the complete absence of formal policing by the state. This may help in the construction of behavioral norms in which perpetrators have a low expectancy of identification, capture, or prosecution. In other cases, some communities in a deeply divided society may have come to expect preferential treatment by law enforcement agencies. For example, a police force may be overwhelmingly recruited from one community and thus reflect that community's political and cultural ethos. This, together with strong kinship links between the police and sections of the community, may result in the view that the risks of prosecution are minor. Breaking the cycle of a social habituation to crime seems particularly problematic given that the introduction of more rigorous policing may not be interpreted as a politically neutral act.

A social environment conducive to crime can suggest community complicity. While the state or international community may label certain activities as criminal, the local community may hold a different, noncriminal, interpretation. For example, cigarette smuggling in Balkan states has few direct or immediately visible victims in the communities that constitute the transit routes. A community may also be inclined to overlook the behavior of some group members because of their wartime service. Profiting from crime may be regarded as a due reward for former combatants who made sacrifices for the cause. Just as community complicity applies to perpetrators, it also extends to victims. A blind eye may be turned to the criminal victimization of members of other groups. Of course, community complicity may not always be voluntary. Those engaged in criminal activities may induce community loyalty, compliance, or passivity through threats and intimidation. What may appear as community ambivalence may in fact be the silence of a community carefully marshaled into obedience.

A third factor specific to post–peace accord societies that may contribute to crime is the presence of significant numbers of former combatants. Ethnonational conflict often results in the mobilization of the population, particularly young adult males, and a consequent distortion of the civilian economy. An end to violent conflict may lead to the downsizing of the security establishment and the disbanding of irregular military forces. In a number of post-accord situations, demobilization programs have attempted to integrate former combatants into the civilian economy via retraining programs and microcredit schemes (see, for example, Gamba 2003). In Mali in 1995–96, for instance, ex-combatants gathered in cantonments, were disarmed ($100 was paid per weapon), and recruited for government jobs, including the armed forces (Poulton and Youssouf 1998, 115–19). The depressed nature of postwar economies means that the private sector is usually unable to accommodate large influxes of labor. Unemployment, underemployment, and poor job prospects beckon many former combatants, making informal, and in some cases illegal, money-making schemes more attractive. As Virginia Gamba notes elsewhere in this volume (see chapter 4), the skills developed by those drawn into the conflict may have little utility in the legitimate economy in the postwar reconstruction phase. Revenue streams that were available during the violent phase of the conflict, for example, diamond mining or banditry, by no means disappear with the declaration of a peace deal.

As important as the mere presence of former combatants are the organizational dynamics within militant organizations. Many militant organizations in ethnonational conflicts are formed on an ad hoc basis, with personnel becoming members for a variety of reasons. While some may be ideologically or politically committed to the cause, others may join for reasons of family, peer pressure, esteem, revenge, or economic gain. In some conflicts, for example, in parts of Uganda and southern Sudan, "membership by kidnap" has been common. As a result, many militant organizations (both insurgent and counterinsurgent) are ripe for fragmentation once the central organizing principle, the ongoing violent conflict, is removed. The pattern of fragmentation may, to some extent, reflect motivations for joining the militant organization, with ideological zealots coalescing around a diehard rump and those motivated by accumulation free to pursue their primary aim unencumbered by politics. But the pattern of fragmentation is unlikely to be so clear-cut, especially if economic circumstances necessitate a more widespread recourse to illegal means of earning a living. Individual and unit specialization during the conflict, geographical location, and kinship connections are also likely to influence involvement in post-accord criminal activities. Matveeva (2002) notes that it is common for criminal gangs to be "organized around ethnic affiliations" and to be based on a "core kinship group," making the task of penetration by law enforcement agencies all the more difficult.

A fourth crime-contributing factor in post-accord societies may be the prevalence of weapons. A common feature of violent ethnonational conflicts has been the spread of small arms.[16] Easily assembled, maintained, concealed, transported, and traded, many of these arms have a long working life. Many peace processes have attempted to institute disarmament programs (see, for example, Boothby 1998). The success of these programs has varied enormously, with many former combatants preferring to hold on to their weapons. Often this is due to political or military calculations: peace may not hold and the weapons may have to be used again. Weapons may also acquire a sociocultural value, and ownership of a gun may have associations of status or be connected with the rites of passage to adulthood. A retention of weapons in a post-accord environment may also have a criminal dimension. In the first instance, many weapons retain an economic value and can be traded. The recycling of weapons from conflict zone to conflict zone is a common feature of contemporary conflict. Second, the weapons can be used in criminal violence. A number of post-accord societies have seen the use of military weapons for criminal purposes, adding a further dimension of violence to criminal behavior and providing arguments against the disarmament and demobilization of state police and military forces.

A fifth factor common in postwar societies that can contribute to high levels of crime is the level and type of post-accord international aid. The post–Cold War period has witnessed a number of large-scale United Nations peacekeeping and peace support operations with state building, physical reconstruction, and political engineering dimensions. The UN operation in Cambodia, for example, cost $2 billion (U.S.) with a further $1.5 billion disbursed in relief and development aid between 1993 and 1998 (ACCORD 1998). Investment in the Balkans by the UN, NATO, the EU, and others has been of gigantic proportions. In the 1995–2000 period, international aid to Bosnia alone amounted to $5.5 billion (U.S.) (International Crisis Group 2001, 1). The sheer scale of investment activities by the international community, together with the type of investment, has created opportunities for corruption. Increasingly, the modus operandi of internationally sponsored development activities has emphasized the delegation of responsibility away from international organizations to international and local nongovernmental organizations (NGOs). Local participation also features heavily in post-accord redevelopment activities. There are good reasons for this, not least the creation of local stakeholders in any peace-building exercise. However, the diffusion of financial and managerial control of development and reconstruction projects can multiply opportunities for corruption.

Perhaps the main factor contributing to crime in postwar societies is uneven economic development. Most postwar societies are chronically poor. Wallensteen and Sollenberg (2000, 636–37 and 2001, 630–31) note that thirteen protracted conflicts terminated between 1998 and 2000. As table 6.1 shows, with the exception of Northern Ireland, all of these societies have a low per capita gross national income for 2000. But these figures mask a much more complex picture in that conflicts are usually located in marginalized regions of states. The income figures in the conflict areas are probably much lower than depicted in the table.

Many post-accord societies stay poor. In 1997 per capita gross domestic product (GDP) in Sierra Leone was $410 (U.S.); in 2000 it had grown to $490. In the same period, Mali's per capita GDP grew by a mere $57 to $797. Other post-accord societies have shown encouraging signs of economic growth (per

TABLE 6.1: PER CAPITA GROSS NATIONAL INCOME IN POST-CONFLICT SOCIETIES, 1998–2000

CONFLICTS TERMINATING IN 1998–2000	PER CAPITA GROSS NATIONAL INCOME IN 2000 (US DOLLARS)
Cambodia	260
Congo-Brazzaville	630
Dagestan	1,660
East Timor	570
Egypt	1,490
Ethiopia	100
Guinea Bissau	180
Kosovo	756–2,995
Lesotho	540
Myanmar	220
Northern Ireland	24,500
Peru	2,100
Tajikistan	170

SOURCE: UNICEF (2002). The figures for Northern Ireland refer to the UK; for Dagestan, Russia; for Kosovo, a range for the former Yugoslavia; for East Timor, Indonesia. The conflict in Myanmar refers to that between the government and the Shan State Army, in Ethiopia between the government and the Somali-based Islamic Union, and in Egypt between the government and the Islamic Association.

capita GDP in Croatia grew from $4,895 to $8,091 between 1997 and 2000), yet the benefits of economic growth may be poorly distributed, and the model of economic growth pursued may not always maximize sustainability.[17]

The list of debilitating economic circumstances usually associated with post-accord societies is extensive: high public debt, underinvestment, unemployment, low revenue collection rates, a weak currency, and a dependency on imports. The often promised "peace dividend" is a rare phenomenon, and most post-accord economies are poorly placed to make advantageous connections with the global economy. A low-technology industrial base, a largely unskilled workforce, poor (possibly war-damaged) infrastructure, and the threat of a return to violence mean that international investment is low. What this translates into at the individual and family level is extreme poverty, a lack of state provision, and few prospects for economic betterment.

Poverty per se is not the major issue in relation to crime. The leap between poverty and crime is a large one, and by no means automatic.[18] Instead, the key is the unevenness of economic development in a postwar context. Wealth and income differentiation are often significant within conflict areas and between those areas that suffered directly from the conflict and those that were relatively unscathed. In a post-accord society the differences in economic status may often follow ethnic cleavages, awarding them a political currency that harks back to the conflict. A dangerous perceptual nexus can develop that links unmet economic needs and perceptions, ethnic politics, and the heritage of violent conflict.

Aside from the six environmental factors reviewed above, peace accords can contribute to crime in more direct ways. The withdrawal or reform of police and security forces can heighten opportunities for crime. Palestinian and Israeli criminal gangs were able to cooperate on car theft following the extension of Palestinian autonomy under the Oslo Accords (Robins 2002, 150–52).

There seems to be a high correlation between the foregoing environmental factors and post-accord societies affected by crime. Most, if not all, of the factors are present in those post-accord societies associated with crime surges, and many of the factors are mutually reinforcing. The factors also seem persistent, largely impervious to quick-fix solutions. If these factors are the long-term legacy of eth-nonational conflict, does this also suggest crime will be a long-term factor?

CONCLUSION AND DISCUSSION

Large-scale crime after the institution of a major peace accord presents government, society, and the international community with an enormous problem. At one level, peace accords must be informed by a certain level of optimism, a recognition that a "fresh start" is required. Postwar transitions normally involve major reform and shrinkage of the state's security apparatus. While involving a good deal of hardhead-ed politics, the new accord may be grounded in plural and communitarian ethics that seek to accommodate difference. Yet all states must retain an authoritarian capability, preferably with popularly agreed upon checks. Postwar polities are fragile and often face concerted threats from spoiler violence. If a peace accord is to survive in the face of such threats, the government (and possibly the international community) will be tempted to use force. The key here is legitimacy and whether the government can claim support from a majority of the community from which the spoiler groups emerge. This debate on the legitimate use of force to enforce a peace settlement has important implications for attempts to tackle crime. If the post–peace accord state retains and uses it authoritarian capability, then it is difficult to protect the state and the peace accord from accusations of political bias. Of vital importance in this regard is the reorganization of the criminal justice system and security sector reform within the context of a peace accord.

A key question remains, however: can post-accord crime threaten the peace? Vickers notes that El Salvador "has been overwhelmed by crime," while Guatemala faces an "epidemic" of crime (1999, 400). Du Toit points out that in South Africa in 1995, 26,637 people were murdered, "more than the number of political fatalities for the entire decade of 1984–1994" (2001, 47). In Dagestan, according to Matveeva, criminal gangs have become so powerful that "The kidnapping of civilians has become a virtually unpunishable offense unless the victim's family can afford to embark on a vendetta" (2002, 377). It is possible to find indications of the pervasiveness of criminality in virtually all post–peace accord societies.

Thus far, crime has not been identified as the major factor contributing to the outright failure of a peace accord. Crime can affect the quality of the peace, however, and contribute to a mood of disaffection that threatens support for the peace accord or a new political dispensation. Crime has been a central and persistent theme in intergroup perceptions that have sustained ethnonational conflicts. The view that a particular out-group is responsible for crime and that the in-group is the likely victim is difficult to erode, regardless of the signing of a peace accord. Perceptions of other groups are often deeply entrenched and, in the case of crime, are liable to be refueled by high-profile assaults or murders. The survival of a peace accord and new political dispensation may rely on a popular concord or an acceptance of the need to give and take. It is here that perceptions of crime and the culpability of out-groups can play a crucial role in undermining this concord. In other words, there is a risk that crime could reenergize ethnic divisions.

Particular elements of a peace accord are liable to be corroded through crime and government and popular reactions to crime. Provisions on human rights and security sector reform could be undermined by government reactions to a crime surge. "Punitive-populism" may take two forms.[19] First, it may encourage a government to follow an authoritarian path in relation to its criminal justice policy and reform of law enforcement agencies—a path that may directly contradict the liberalizing intentions and provisions of a peace accord. Second, it may encourage sections of the population to take matters into their own hands through vigilantism and a privatization of security. The PAGAD (People Against Gangsterism and Drugs) movement and rapid response security firms in South Africa, although often serving different clients, both reflect a lack of faith in the ability of the government to provide civilian security.

While particular elements of a peace accord may be undermined, for example, commitments to human rights or security sector reform, crime may present a more general threat in eroding support for a peace process and accord. Although there have been a significant number of major peace initiatives, sustained peace processes, and peace treaties over the past decade, many peace processes have introduced a dysfunctional, strained peace. While most group-on-group violence may have ceased and major institutional reform may have been introduced, many post-accord societies suffer from a range of debilitating problems. Whether in Tajikistan or Bosnia, problems include illiberal democracy, structural corruption, the persistence of on-the-ground sectarian tensions, and economic underdevelopment. Peace processes risk becoming protracted and skewed to the extent that they prioritize the wishes of the international community and local elites ahead of the vast bulk of the population. Essentially, a peace initiative may fail to deal with the underlying causes of the conflict.

The key danger is the sapping of the confidence of the propeace constituency and the failure to fulfill the expectations of the population at large. If people's material conditions do not improve as a result of a transition from war to peace, then it is difficult for them to become stakeholders in that peace. Fundamentally, people may undermine an accord by removing electoral support from those parties supporting the peace agreement. Crime can play an enormous role in shaking public confidence in peace. This is particularly the case because it can have an insidious quality that allows it to become suffused with identity-related grievances at the root of many ethnonational conflicts. While unlikely to jeopardize a peace process on its own, crime can contribute to the popular notion that peace is not working.

NOTES

1. *Independent* (London), January 21, 2002, and *Guardian* (London), December 31, 2000.

2. The United Nations Development Program (UNDP) has championed the notion of human security, particularly with the publication of its 1994 Human Development Report, *New Dimensions on Human Security.*

3. An excellent discussion of transnational organized crime (TOC) is contained in Farer (1999).

4. As evidence of the political interest in organized crime, it was the focus of a high-level UN conference in December 2000, an EU-Russian agreement in April 2001, and an Interpol conference in May 2001, and featured in former U.S. secretary of state Anthony Lake's security "nightmares" as told in his *Six Nightmares* (2001). Like other real and supposed post–Cold War threats (for example, illegal immigration, weapons of mass destruction, rogue states, and Islamic fundamentalism), the dangers of transnational organized crime have become conflated with "terrorism."

5. For an insight into crime in postwar Berlin and the role of U.S. troops in the informal economy, see Ruffner (2002).

6. The phenomenon of "spoiler" violence in peace processes is discussed in

Stedman (1997). Darby examines continuing violence in the context of peace initiatives in *The Effects of Violence on Peace Processes* (2001).

7. Accounts of the dynamics of peace processes can be found in Darby and Mac Ginty (2000 and 2003). See also Stedman, Rothchild, and Cousens (2002).

8. The overlap between the military and civilian spheres forms a major part of Mary Kaldor's (1999) characterization of "new wars."

9. This is not to say that these activities do not, or cannot, form part of military-on-military encounters.

10. The legacy of this pattern of ethnic conflict accompanied by theft was witnessed by the author during fieldwork in Croatia (December 2000) and Bosnia Herzegovina (December 2002).

11. The issue of perceptions of violence in deeply divided societies is discussed in Mac Ginty (2001).

12. See, for example, "UN Worried at Rise in Lynchings in Guatemala," June 22, 1998, and "Two Stoned to Death in Guatemala," May 1, 2000, both from BBC News Web site (http://news.bbc.co.uk/).

13. Although not related to a post-accord society, Harnischfeger (2003) provides a chilling insight into the complicity of government in institutionalized vigilantism in Nigeria.

14. In 2002 it was reported that a woman was raped every twenty-six seconds in South Africa. "South African Men March Against Rape," November 20, 2002, BBC News Web site (http://news.bbc.co.uk/).

15. Variations in obedience to the law within different areas of the same state may add a further complication.

16. The need for microdisarmament is discussed in De Clerq (1999).

17. The 1997 figures are taken from the 1999 Human Development Report "Globalization with a Human Face" and the 2000 figures from the 2002 Human Development Report "Deepening Democracy in a Fragmented World" (UNICEF 1997, 2002).

18. Indeed McIlwaine notes that "rates of crime are still lower in developing countries compared with developed nations, although they are increasing much faster in the South, and are more violent in the North" (1999, 454).

19. Edwards and Gill (2002) expand on this issue in relation to organized crime.

TIMOTHY D. SISK

Political Violence and Peace Accords

Searching for the Silver Lining

Between April and June 1994 the most devastating spasm of violence in the post–Cold War era occurred in Rwanda, where in the genocidal frenzy in that country some 800,000 died in 100 days. Among all the considerations of complex underlying causes and precipitants of the Rwanda genocide, clearly one significant stimulus of the violence was the conclusion by moderates in the government and rebel forces of a comprehensive peace accord to end a four-year civil war in that country, the Arusha Agreement of August 1993.[1] As the Rwandan case demonstrates, convulsions of violence are often closely and directly related to the process of peacemaking; violence and negotiation are inherently and complexly interrelated.

In this case, the clinching of a peace agreement provided a context in which new violence —ostensibly to prevent its full implementation—was perpetrated. Indeed, the principal accelerator of the Rwandan genocide was the downing of President Juvenal Habyarimana's airplane on April 6, 1994, as it approached the runway in Kigali; Habyarimana was returning from follow-up peace talks in Arusha, Tanzania, on implementation of the peace agreement. The crash killed Habyarimana and the president of neighboring Burundi as well. Hutu ethnic extremists in the government opposed to the Arusha peace talks are believed to have assassinated the president because they feared the concessions he made would jeopardize their control of the country's armed forces. The horrid, orchestrated violence that ensued quickly negated the lofty aims of the Arusha talks; eventually, military victory by the then-rebel ethnic Tutsi–led Rwanda Patriotic Front ended the genocide and terminated the civil war.

In Rwanda and elsewhere, political violence by extremists opposed to peace destroys efforts by more moderate parties to de-escalate conflict through negotiation. Whether in Rwanda, Angola, Chechnya, Burundi, Côte d'Ivoire, Israel-Palestine, Liberia, Sri Lanka, or Aceh (Indonesia), to name a few recent instances, violence after peace accords can bring down fragile talks to end the conflict by making the demands of disarmament and demobilization untenable.

Ongoing violence clearly has deleterious effects on peacemaking even as ostensibly well-intentioned political leaders seek to end killing by negotiating the terms of a sustainable peace. Peacemaking efforts are invariably difficult—virtually insurmountable in many instances—precisely because, ironically, levels of violence *increase* while parties are gathered around the negotiating table. Furthermore, political violence usually continues into the implementation phases of peacemaking as opponents of peace launch last-ditch efforts to prevent its terms from becoming reality. Major turning points—both breakthroughs and breakdowns—in a peace process are often accompanied by sharp upsurges in violence precisely because talking and fighting by protagonists in civil wars are so closely related.

Violence and negotiation are part of an overall strategy of conflict that includes threat, persuasion, coercion, and defection (Schelling 1980). Political violence, both as a prelude to talks and during them, is a "beyond-the-table tactic" that is used by extremist forces that reject peace (as in Rwanda) and by the negotiating parties themselves as a bargaining chip. In fact, violence is an integral part of the overall bargaining process in contemporary civil wars. Complex relationships between violence and negotiation in contemporary internal conflicts are omnipresent, with recursive effects. Violence affects negotiation, and negotiation events affect levels and types of violence. Commonly, as in Rwanda, violence unambiguously undermines attempts to reach a negotiated settlement, reinforcing the commitment of adversaries to military methods of achieving their objectives.[2]

Can there be silver linings in post-accord violence in which the violence spurs the protagonists to move more assertively to implement peace? The answer is sometimes; in some situations sharp upsurges of violence at key turning points in the peace process have reinforced the resolve of negotiators to enter talks or to press ahead with ongoing negotiations and clinch an agreement on peace. In

South Africa violence during the late stages of the negotiation processes to end apartheid—particularly attempts by rejectionists to derail the elections of April 1994—tended to affirm the resolve of moderates committed to implementation of the negotiated settlement (Sisk 1995, 243; Sisk 1993). With their proverbial noses bloodied from the fight, upsurges in violence might induce those engaged in organized conflict to pull back from the brink of even greater violence.

Some crises of violence, with their human death, suffering, and destruction, do have a silver lining in their stormy clouds—they compel protagonists to de-escalate in anticipation of even more costly catastrophes and crises. This chapter seeks to identify some of the ways in which political violence affects peace processes, in particular, how the incentives for violence for different parties change over the course of protracted negotiations. In mapping the incentives for violence and the social psychology of seeking peace, perhaps we can identify the factors in which post-accord violence can—in an ironic way—serve as a catalyst for the eventual disappearance of violence. The chapter ends with the difficult yet compelling finding that implementing peace in civil wars requires parties and external conciliators to anticipate violence, seek to mitigate its effects on negotiation, and press ahead with implementation of peace pacts despite the fact that violence may be escalating on the ground.

VIOLENCE AS A STRATEGY OF CONFLICT

Dramatic peace processes in deadly ethnic conflicts have unfolded since the end of the Cold War. Some have succeeded in ending the bloodletting through negotiation, while other attempts to negotiate settlements have palpably failed and the fighting resumed; still others are ongoing (Darby and Mac Ginty 2000). Research on these peace processes shows that modern wars are more likely to terminate at the negotiating table than on the battlefield (Wallensteen and Sollenberg 2001; King 1997).[3] These recent peace processes already yield a poignant lesson: the initial silencing of the guns and the opening of formal talks does not mean that political violence will end. As John Darby asserts, "Even when political violence is ended by a cease-fire, it reappears in other forms to threaten the evolving peace process" (Darby 2001, 13–14). Darby identifies four main categories of violence: violence by the state, violence by militants, violence in the community, and the emergence of new violence-related issues during the negotiations (Darby 2001, 37–66). This typology provides an insightful perspective on the underlying sources of violence in terms of its origins and effects on issues such as negotiations. Darby argues that violence early in the peace process makes negotiation more vulnerable to its deleterious effects, especially in those

particularly volatile moments just after a ceasefire and before substantive negotiations have made much progress.

Far from ending the violence, peace talks generate powerful incentives for
some parties to the conflict to actually foment *more* violence to influence what
happens at the negotiating table—to maximize bargaining positions, to weaken
opponents, to prevent being sidelined, or to sabotage the talks altogether. Such
violence is part of a strategy of conflict;[4] killing, threat, intimidation, and the like
are a "beyond-the-table" tactic, perpetrated by those who are party to the talks
(such as a government's security forces) and by "rejectionists" (such as ultrana-
tionalists opposed to ending the conflict through negotiation) alike. While not
all instances of violence may be calculated and strategic—there is a pathological
dimension to acts of violence (Rothchild and Groth 1995)—certain acts of violence are clearly strategic in their objectives.[5] Violence is the main type of punitive tactic, or sanction, in a bargaining relationship.[6] Equally important to analyze are threats to employ violence and related tactics such as bluffs. As a punitive tactic, violence is often fomented in response to the inherent incentive structure of the bargaining processes. This finding suggests that much of the violence
that accompanies peace processes is instrumental (Höglund 2001).

After negotiations begin and even after initial, interim, or comprehensive
peace accords are reached, violence and the threats of resorting to violence continue to affect the scope, pace, and agenda of talks during this tenuous phase of
conflict de-escalation. What happens on the street—continuing military engagements, terrorist bombings, assassinations and hit squads, deadly riots, security
force atrocities, and faction fighting—is related to what happens at the table, and
what happens at the table is related to what happens on the street. Under what
conditions does beyond-the-table political violence cause talks to derail, and
under what conditions does it reinforce the initial motivations of the parties to
seek a negotiated exit to the conflict? The success or failure of peace talks often
depends on whether the negotiations can progress in the face of ongoing, even
intensified, violence.

Much of the impetus for increasing political violence during peace talks is
found in the deep and profound uncertainty that negotiations bring about. The
utter uncertainty that characterizes tenuous peace processes—will parties lose at
the table what they have not lost on the battlefield?—generates incentives for
some parties to foment violence in order to prevent their fears from coming true.
The use of violence is often reflective of a sense of certainty of power: if we have
weapons and use them, we can protect ourselves or attack our opponent. The
rationale of the protagonists in civil wars—government security forces and rebels
alike—is similar: if a peace agreement requires us to disarm or otherwise become
vulnerable, we will lose our ability to protect ourselves. A certain violent equilib-

rium, or "hurting stalemate," is perceived to be better than the vulnerabilities of an uncertain peace (Zartman 2000).

In analyzing violence that accompanies peace processes, key questions are whether elites purposefully manipulate and organize violence, whether it emanates from a more spontaneous, mass dissatisfaction with peace efforts, or whether midlevel elites (local party bosses, ground-level militia or military commanders, party-aligned "warlords," etc.) who resist demobilization from conflict are primarily responsible for fanning the flames. A critical issue is whether elites can persuade or "deliver" their organizations and the constituencies upon which they depend, and what it means for elites to demobilize their combatants and communities after so many years of mobilization for conflict. That is, it is easier to understand how elites can mobilize organizations and constituencies for violence than to understand how they can demobilize them when the moment for peace arrives (Duffy and Frensley 1989). For this reason, processes of demobilization, disarmament, and reintegration (sometimes known as DDR) that address the needs of former combatants have emerged as front-burner tasks in postwar environments (Darby 2001, 66–75).

A critical variable is the expected culpability of midlevel elites in fomenting political violence to influence the negotiations, as well as the relevant strengths of moderates versus hardliners *within* each group, faction, or party.[7] Intragroup and intraorganizational differences—along a hard line–moderate continuum—deserve analytical priority over intergroup and interorganizational animosity in understanding the propensity toward violence during negotiations. Darby rightly refers to this type of violence as "family feuding" (Darby 2001, 57–61).

Political violence can undermine the basis of negotiations by affecting public opinion about the viability of talks and the true intentions of opposing communities, by diminishing elite confidence and trust about the intent of their adversaries, or by demonstrating that elites at the table may not be able to deliver their constituencies. On the other hand, lack of progress in talks may lead certain parties to foment violence. That is, the relationships are *recursive*—violence may impede progress, and lack of progress may stimulate violence. This makes the violence-negotiation nexus theoretically and methodologically challenging to capture and explain, but it heightens its appeal as a research problem.

Sharp upsurges in overall levels of political violence, or critical events such as a high-profile terrorist bombing, assassination, or deadly riot, are invariably critical turning points in negotiation processes.[8] That is, events such as these force those at the negotiating table to make critical choices, essentially whether to recoil and return to the fight, or hunker down, continue talking, and weather the political storm.[9] In sum, dramatic political violence is *crisis inducing* in that the parties are required to make critical choices on whether and how the peace process should progress. Following a crisis-inducing event, will the peace process be derailed? Under what conditions does crisis-inducing political violence prompt disputants to retract from talks, and under what conditions does it prompt disputants to continue talking as the way to ultimately settle the issues that are the underlying causes of violence?

MAPPING INCENTIVES FOR VIOLENCE IN PEACE PROCESSES

To understand violence that occurs after an initial, interim, or comprehensive peace accord is signed, it is important to evaluate the type of accord that has been reached and the phase of negotiation in which the parties find themselves. Different stages of negotiation incur different risks, and an analysis of post-settlement violence requires this important context to be taken into account. As suggested in the introduction to this volume, peace agreements can be initial commitments to talk, cease-fires, interim agreements, or comprehensive pacts. Recent research even refers to the notion of "post-settlement settlements," or bargaining that continues well into the implementation phase (du Toit 2003). Post-accord violence is a stage in a process model of conflict termination from prenegotiation, in which parties informally consult before taking the risks of going public in open, formal talks, through to sustainable peace (Saunders 1991). For evaluating post-accord violence, the framework should account for the latter stages of bargaining, well after the ink is dry on a formal settlement, and into the "peace-building" phase to include the critical issues of sustainability of negotiated settlements (Stedman, Rothchild, and Cousens 2002). If a negotiated settlement is not durable, is it a settlement after all?

The essential premise of a phases approach is that during the course of negotiations, parties move incrementally toward a settlement, staking positions, making concessions, linking issues, formulating agreements, and structuring the implementation process.[10] The settlement, which culminates but does not end the bargaining process, represents the convergence point of the parties' positions on a wide array of issues, from disarmament to elections. In protracted, violent conflicts it is no surprise that single, comprehensive agreements are not possible. Parties in violent conflicts need sustained and detailed negotiation processes to work through the various stages of reconciling their differences in order to feel that the outcome of talks—inevitably less than their ideal outcomes—is fair, the best possible solution from their vantage point, and sufficiently strong to protect their vital interests. Finally, a sequential process of give and take can, over time, allow parties to discover a just outcome to their disputes that may not have been evident from the outset of talks.

The phases approach is adopted for this framework of analysis because it highlights a central fact: as a peace process moves from initial escalation through various stages to a settlement and eventually its implementation, the incentive structure for violence by parties engaged in the negotiation and rejectionists changes dramatically. As the peace process unfolds, new information and opportunities arise for parties to influence the structure and direction of the talks and, consequently, its outcomes. The changing incentive structure of the conflict is more fully highlighted below, where the general characteristics of the various phases are outlined and propositions regarding the incentives and disincentives for violence for different types of parties to a conflict are posited.

The essential point is that conceiving of a peace process as a series of phases linked by turning points allows for a fruitful analysis of the strategic choices by parties about when to fight, when to talk, when to threaten and bluff, what type of arguments to make to justify their actions, when to concede, and, ultimately, when to settle.[11] With this framework, the special problems of post-accord violence can be more carefully delineated.

PHASE I: VIOLENCE AND CONFLICT ESCALATION

There is a longstanding differentiation in the literature on violence between structural causes of violence and proximate causes. That is, while the true *causes* of a conflict are invariably difficult to pinpoint, the sequence of events by which they escalate is more amenable to identification and analysis. A useful conceptual tool for identifying the outbreak of violent conflict is to focus on a specific event or series of events that trigger the outbreak of violence. Conflict triggers can include provocative acts by political leaders, failed elections, abrupt changes in the regional security environment, or violent upsurges such as riots or spontaneous uprisings (Hewitt 1993). The 1992 referendum on Bosnian independence from the former Yugoslavia was *the* trigger that ignited the civil war.[12]

An important point is that once violence breaks out in an internal conflict, the violence itself generates new incentives for its perpetuation. There are both psychological and strategic reasons for this. Psychologically, studies have shown that participants in violence become committed to it as a way of life—the "cult of violence" (Taylor 1991). Strategically, governments have an incentive to show firmness, resolve, and staying power in the face of resistance and terror, and challengers have in interest in demonstrating their power to cause further instability and for stating demands that, if granted, proved that the turn to violence was warranted. That is, parties become *committed* to their course of action, and as violence intensifies so too does the commitment. Thus, the turn to violence and its escalation creates "social traps," or cycles of violence, in which parties find it difficult, if not impossible, to escape. The culture of violence, political as well as criminal or social, may last well into the post-settlement phase.

PHASE II: THE MUTUALLY HURTING STALEMATE

The arrival at a "mutually hurting" stalemate suggests that parties have reached the point where further escalation is self-defeating, and indeed further pursuit of the conflict imposes greater costs than benefits. In theory, all parties could potentially gain from cooperation, but (similar to the prisoners' dilemma game) their immediate incentives mitigate against such cooperation. Moreover, the role of external parties in contemporary internal conflicts often reinforces conditions of stalemate by providing cross-border resources to parties (such as support by neighboring regimes of insurgents), by enhancing their legitimacy, or by simply participating in the open international arms market.

Parties in internal conflicts may control different spheres of power, roughly equal in the balance. Moreover, states may have an existence and other interests independent of the conflict, with limited resources and interest to devote to decisively winning an armed struggle. On the other hand, insurgents may devote their all to the conflict; their very survival depends upon it. In sum, the government may enjoy an asymmetry of military power, whereas the insurgents may enjoy an asymmetry of commitment. This is what Alexander George has termed an "asymmetry of motivation" (George 1994, 1993). The cost-benefit calculations of further fighting may be markedly different for different parties depending on their level of devotion to the conflict. In sum, violence may persist even though it is unlikely to succeed in achieving its strategic aims because of the parties' misperception of their own capabilities.

PHASE III: PRENEGOTIATION AND THE RIPE MOMENT

The mutually hurting stalemate is a necessary structural condition for the onset of a negotiation process in internal conflicts, but it is certainly not a sufficient one. In different internal conflicts, a mutually hurting stalemate may "objectively" exist with remarkably different levels of political violence. The condition is resistant to measurement in terms of actual levels, deaths in political violence as a proportion of a population, or by measuring the time in which disputants are engaged in a conflict without the real prospect of decisive de-escalation.[13] The question of "When does a mutually hurting stalemate hurt *enough* to turn intransigence into opportunities for accommodation?" is one measured only in terms of the perceptions of the parties. They must commonly share a sense of urgency to bring the stalemate to an end through decisive de-escalation.

The ebb and flow of violence is a critical factor in the creation of a ripe moment. Is a conflict ripe when the level of violence is expected to go higher, when it reaches an apex, or when it begins to decline? Are there possibilities for conflicts to be ripe "early," without a low threshold of violence, or "late" and even "very late," that is, after very significant levels of violence? The mutually hurting stalemate notion implies that a moment is ripe when levels of political violence flatten out, or reach a plateau, but may sharply escalate if action to de-escalate is not taken. The perceptual changes necessary to turn stalemate into ripeness is a fundamental change that can occur following a dramatic upsurge in violence, for example, a planned or unplanned escalation, often some dramatic event such as a costly but indecisive battle or incident of mass terror. The crisis may have entailed significant mutual loss but did not move the conflict toward resolution. Moreover, parties may alter their perceptions about the costs of continued violent confrontation and the potential benefits of negotiation when they anticipate an impending crisis, which will also impose considerable costs without tangible gain.

PHASE IV: PRELIMINARY FORMAL NEGOTIATION

The movement from prenegotiation to open, formal negotiation is signaled by the parties' first implicit or explicit peace accord: "going public" with their intent to replace fighting with talking. An announcement to the public that a party is negotiating with a bitter adversary is a major turning point in the de-escalation process.[14] This turning point signals, more than any other, that political leaders are willing to accept the inevitable risks and costs associated with direct negotiations, such as charges from immoderate rejectionist parties of appeasement, betrayal, or capitulation, in pursuit of the still-unrealized benefits of a negotiated settlement. Public acknowledgement that a regime or insurgent group will together seek a negotiated settlement radically transforms the landscape of a conflict and significantly alters the incentive structure for violence. The move is especially risky for governments, who open themselves up to charges of negotiating with terrorists, in effect "rewarding" violence.[15]

The onset of open negotiation unleashes a new, uncertain interregnum. The status quo of violent conflict without end is transformed into a situation in which the old order is likely to be changed, yet the parameters of the post–negotiated settlement order have not been established. The period after the immediate onset of negotiations raises many questions about the period of transition, the opportunities and dangers it may pose, and for how long, but also about the terms of a settlement and the many problems that are as yet unresolved. Precisely because not just the security forces, but all segments of society, are deeply uncertain about their futures after the onset of formal negotiations in internal conflicts, the preliminary negotiation, post–initial agreement phase of a peace process is a highly unsettled and turbulent period.

The preliminary formal negotiation phase is also marked by the changing dynamics of coalition making. Erstwhile enemies on the battlefield, such as a government and insurgent group, find themselves in an implicit coalition defending the choice for negotiation, reorienting their rhetoric toward moderation and compromise, and articulating the benefits of negotiation and the costs of continued violent conflict. At the same time, they remain adversaries in the negotiation, with widely divergent aims and hopes for the ensuing talks. Importantly, the relationships among parties at the table are marked by both cooperation (as partners in talks) *and* competition. Rejectionist parties, or spoilers, from all sides of the divide have an implicit interest in fomenting violence to derail talks. By stoking the flames of conflict, rejectionist parties seek to demonstrate that negotiations are untenable and that military victory remains the sole solution to the conflict (Stedman 1997).

In all cases of deep conflict, a critical question is whether being at the table is a tactical move by parties—subduing the opponent through other nonviolent means—or a genuine search for a mutually beneficial solution. The test is whether the parties progress and reach preliminary agreements on the cessation of violence or whether the negotiation process fails to progress.

PHASE V: SETTLEMENT NEGOTIATIONS

As the talks move from security issues to substantive issues, such as the division of territory or the nature, form, and structure of the state, it is a signal that parties have entered the phase of negotiation in which the actual terms of a settlement are being thrashed out. Parties in internal conflicts face essentially two choices for the settlement of underlying disputes: "separation," that is, political divorce or secession, and sharing, or creating the structures for living together (Sisk 1996). The purpose of a substantive settlement is to reconstitute "normal" politics in a society and to create new, mutually beneficial rules of the political game. Ultimately, parties in a negotiation process to resolve deep-seated conflict arrive at institutional solutions: rules and procedures through which to arbitrate their differences peacefully in parliament rather than violently on the street.

Settlements can be initial, interim, or comprehensive. As noted above, initial settlements are really agreements to talk. In interim settlements, parties are able to arrive at some basis for reconstituting normal politics but cannot agree on, or prefer to defer, highly sensitive or unresolved issues. Interim settlements are usually partial agreements, whereas final settlements purport to be comprehensive in scope. All settlements seek to formalize patterns of interaction, and in this respect they seek to establish new incentive structures in their own right, resolving some of the uncertainty about the new rules of the game, which characterizes earlier phases of the peace process. In many cases they are package proposals that resolve multiple issues simultaneously by linking them. Comprehensive settlements are more ambitious: they seek to definitively resolve a conflict for the indefinite future, with provisions to address immediate and long-term issues and to fully resolve all outstanding issues in contention; often, such settlements take the form of new constitutions for deeply divided societies that seek to replace open war on the streets with managed conflict in the form of democratic institutions.

Importantly, the formal substantive phase of a peace process—especially as this phase nears an end and a settlement emerges on the horizon—strongly affects the incentives for violence. Once comprehensive settlements are reached, another significant turning point occurs. For parties to a conflict, the incentives for violence ostensibly fall away all together. The further employment of violence becomes illegitimate; disputes are not to be resolved in the streets but rather within the newly created institutions envisaged by the accord. For rejectionist spoilers, however, there may be one last-ditch opportunity to reverse the pattern of accommodation: prevent the terms of the accord from being implemented.

PHASE VI: IMPLEMENTATION

Clearly, reaching a comprehensive peace accord is not the end of the process; violence can erupt with a vengeance even after moderates have agreed to a comprehensive settlement. The implementation phase of peace processes can be just as volatile, just as violence-ridden, as early phases of the process. Successful implementation requires translating the terms of agreement on paper into real institutions and practices that reorient politics from the street to the parliament. Usually, however, implementation of settlements in internal conflicts does not occur in a vacuum. Normally, earlier interim agreements or security pacts have been put into place, leaving behind them both lessons from the past and structures for cooperation.

Following Ball (1996), the post-settlement phase can itself be analyzed in terms of its constituent phases: an initial period of security, a second period of institution building and elections, and a third period of long-term reconstruction and reconciliation in the pursuit of sustainable peace. The most extensive look at these various components of post-settlement peace building is *Ending Civil Wars: The Implementation of Peace Agreements* (Stedman, Rothchild, and Cousens 2002). One of the most enduring findings from this and other studies (such as du Toit 2001) tells us that societies emerging from civil wars have exceptionally weak states with little ability to provide essential human security, wrecked economies, and devastated communities and civil societies. The essential long-term goal of peace building is to create a viable, capable state sufficiently in touch with its society to be able to manage social conflicts through institutions of bargaining, consensus building, legislating, and gaining compliance from its population. Centrally, violence occurs to the extent it must through the coercive capacities of a legitimate state that has the support of its people (du Toit 2003). Indeed, this finding is reflected in the work of World Bank economists, who argue that a capable state is the key to exiting conflict "traps" (Collier 2003).

For the purposes of this analysis, and following Darby (2001), after comprehensive peace agreements have been reached, four types of post-settlement violence can emerge.

- Defection violence by parties to the accord that experience a perverse kind of "buyer's remorse" and subsequently use violence to undermine the pact even though they have agreed to abide by its terms. An example of such defection violence is the return to the battlefield by the UNITA rebel faction, led by Jonas Savimbi, after narrowly losing a post-settlement presidential election in 1992.
- Spoiler violence by those who oppose implementation of the accord and seek to destroy the moderate coalition that has emerged. The Rwanda case cited in the introduction is a case in point, as is the tragic bombing in Omagh that followed on the heels of the Good Friday/Belfast Agreement in Northern Ireland (see Darby 2001, esp. 96–97; and Stedman 1997).
- Community violence, such as ongoing ethnic or social tensions that produce spontaneous tensions over turf, control over resources or livelihoods, or resistance by former combatants to the terms of disarmament or demobilization. In South Africa, despite a number of interim settlements to be included in a comprehensive agreement in June 1992, known as the National Peace Accord, to manage community-level violence, tensions among former anti-apartheid activists, the police, and opposition parties led to some 14,000 deaths over the course of the country's turbulent peace process (see Gastrow 1995). Other studies show how political violence during the time of struggle transforms into criminal violence in the post-settlement era (see chapter 6 in this volume).

- PARTY-POLITICAL VIOLENCE, especially in the context of inaugural post-settlement elections. Whether rejectionist parties choose to fight accommodation from within the new system (as the Pan-Africanist Congress did in South Africa), or whether they boycott it and seek its demise from without (as the Khmer Rouge did in Cambodia), is in part a matter of the terms under which the election will be held. Thus, the electoral system is a key incentive structure that affects the propensity for rejectionists to foment violence. If a rejectionist party believes it can win a few seats in the new parliament, rather than being completely excluded from the new system, this incentive may be enough to widen the base of the peace process and bring in those with the capacity to "spoil."[16]

Finally, settlements in internal conflicts contain the inherent problems of longer-term enforceability and compliance. When the inaugural election is over and the UN peacekeepers leave, there is no external party to further guarantee the accord (Walter 2002). For this reason, Wagner writes, "One of the disadvantages of a negotiated settlement is that, because no combatant is able to disarm its adversaries, a settlement requires that all the adversaries retain some semblance of their organizational identities after the war, even if they are disarmed. While such an agreement may facilitate the ending of one civil war, it may also facilitate the outbreak of the next" (1993, 261).

Thus, when a peace process "ends" is as ambiguous a question as when it begins. The transformation of a regime and the inculcation of new values of compromise and coexistence after a bitter and often protracted conflict are difficult and long-term tasks. Civil wars leave economic and environmental catastrophes in their wake, legacies of enmity that require years and even decades of purposeful socioeconomic development to address. The underlying disputes in an internal conflict may not even be resolved at the end of a peace process, just managed. Nevertheless, the basis for violent opposition to a regime falls away as the new order is consolidated and the incentives for achieving political aims peacefully predominantly emerge, while the incentives for violence may fall away altogether. Whether the new order will be durable is a question of whether the explicit commitment to accommodation can be broadened and deepened over time, lessening the underlying conditions that have fueled the conflict in the first place.

SEARCHING FOR THE SILVER LINING

Can post-accord violence reinforce peace? When do the storm clouds of violence contain a silver lining, in that the violence itself serves as a stimulus to progress in moving progressively toward peace? Rather than pursuing an elusive

notion of success in negotiating peace, a more modest and realistic goal is to identify those conditions that lead to *progress* through the various phases of conflict de-
escalation.[17] Identifying the variables that lead to progress in bargaining can help
identify those conditions and instances in which violence can stimulate parties to
move forward in peace talks rather than retreat back into the relative certainty, however painful, of violent confrontation. Identifying the ways in which violence can
lead to progress also allows for the articulation of policy prescriptions for local proponents of peace and international mediators bolstering implementation of peace
accords.

VIOLENCE, CRISES, AND AVERSION

Under certain conditions, and at particular moments, violence can spur a negotiation process toward peace. The principal mechanism for finding a silver lining
appears to be essentially one of understanding the social psychology of violent conflicts: revulsion, shock, and aversion. Revulsion is the public disgust with the wan-
ton consequences of conflict that produces horrific human death. Shock is the real-
ization of why it happens and perhaps recognition of how intractable the conflict
may be. Aversion is the hope that through further conciliation, compromise, and
bargaining such events can be avoided in the future. For progress toward peace to
occur, the leaders and populations of societies in deep conflict most be motivated—
by disgust, fear, and hope—to avoid an outcome of unending violent encounter that
will be worse in comparison to the risky terms of a peace agreement.

Progress in reducing violence and creating peace through negotiation occurs
when parties pass through recognizable stages or phases of negotiation, from preliminary talks to the successful and sustainable implementation of a comprehensive accord. This is not to suggest, however, that in today's turbulent peace
processes there are not collapses, setbacks, and backsliding of peace negotiations
at every stage or phase of talks. Over time, the tangible economic and social
incentives for peace that are generated by cooperation overtake the lingering
incentives for violence. When may costly political violence have a silver lining
effect in the search for peace? In other words, can the crises that violent encounters produce spur the protagonists in conflict toward greater cooperation? The
following factors seem to be most closely associated with forward momentum in
post-settlement negotiations; each factor is illustrated by an example drawn
from recent experience.

SYMMETRY OF POWER. The perception of a relative balance of power among disputants produces progress toward negotiated settlements.[18] Conversely, profound asymmetries in balance of power relationships impede progress unless one

side is asymmetrically motivated; in many instances, the state has superior power relative to rebel factions, but the rebels are more single-minded in their pursuit of the conflict. After some two decades of civil war, the protagonists in Sri Lanka began serious peace talks in February 2002, mediated by Norway's Foreign Ministry, that sealed an initial ceasefire and launched an extended bargaining process to resolve the territorial and minority rights dispute. While the government forces clearly emerged as militarily more capable, the rebel Tamil Tigers possessed a commitment to the fight—and resources from abroad—that ultimately produced a classic symmetry of effective power. Once the government realized its inability to escalate out of the conflict, and the Tigers realized their inability to achieve their secessionist aims through violence, progress was attained in the form of the LTTE unilateral ceasefire and the initial success of the ceasefire accord. By the end of 2003, post-accord violence from spoiler factions had not yet derailed the talks, although progress in comprehensive settlement negotiations has stymied.

INTERNAL PARTY COHERENCE. Internal party coherence produces greater progress toward negotiated settlements, although in instances where all sides to a conflict lack cohesion, fragmented or divided parties can produce progress. Progress is impeded when one side is coherent and capable but other sides are divided or fragmented. Multiple attempts to negotiate an end to the Kashmir conflict have been stymied by the incoherence among the Kashmiri militants, who are fractured into multiple parties with an umbrella organization (the All-Parties Hurriyat Conference) that thus far has been ineffective in forging an effective coalition for peace. Although there are many other internal and interstate reasons why the Kashmir conflict has been resistant to progress at the negotiating table despite some initial ceasefire agreements, at least one factor has been the lack of internal party coherence on the Kashmiri militant side.

IDEOLOGICAL COMMITMENT. When any party to a negotiation is highly committed to a rigid ideology or ethnonationalist myth, progress in negotiation is impeded. A key determination is whether the justification for violence is cast in such a way as to be instrumental, not essentialist (or maximal), in its aims. Of all the ideologically committed parties in internal conflict, some appear to be ideologically incapable of rearticulating their goals to envisage making peace with their foes. Exemplary in this regard are those elements of the former Taliban in Afghanistan whose Islamist views prevent possible inclusion in the postwar political institutions established by the 2001 Bonn agreement and subsequent accords among more moderate Afghani factions.

CULPABILITY IN VIOLENCE. When a party to a negotiation process is perceived as culpable with regard to a specific violent incident, it has the effect of impeding progress in negotiation. When parties not participating in the negotiations (that is, "outbidder" or rejectionist parties or individuals) are considered culpable, or when parties to a negotiation are perceived (by international actors, for example) as equally culpable, incidents of political violence can reinforce pressures on negotiating parties to progress toward a settlement. Organized or group violence inhibits progress less than random violence perpetrated by individuals. If violence is clearly the result of actions by spoilers, moderates can be bolstered when public revulsion at the horror of an act of violence undermines support for the spoilers. Following the Omagh tragedy of 1998, mentioned above, the public and moderate elites rallied around the Good Friday/Belfast Agreement, and broad support among republicans for violent opposition to continued British rule in the disputed province rapidly evaporated. There was deep revulsion at the consequences of this gruesome bombing. As Darby writes, "Violence, or rather spoiler violence, had become temporarily unfashionable" (2001, 97).

UNCERTAINTY OF OUTCOMES. Disputants engaged in negotiation, and those rejecting negotiation, may deliberately foment violence as a response to the uncertainty that the onset of structured talks unleashes. The more uncertain the situation, that is, the less the specific outcomes of talks are identified and articulated, the greater the level of violence and the likelihood that violence will impede progress. Among all the causes of violence in the post-Oslo environment in the Israeli-Palestinian context, the uncertainty of the "final status" issues has been an impetus to "create facts on the ground," often through the use of violence. For this reason, the alternative Geneva Accord of October 2003 (reached by moderate, unofficial Israeli and Palestinian negotiators) seeks to reverse the sequence of events by resolving final status issues first—especially the demarcation of borders and the disposition of the settlements issues—as a way to remove some incentives for such violence.

TIMING. Violence at an early stage of talks (during prenegotiation or preliminary formal negotiation) disrupts and delays progress toward a settlement more than violence at later stages of talks. However, violence overtly fomented by parties to a negotiation at a late stage of talks impedes progress. Violence by rejectionists at a late stage of the process tends to reinforce moderates' commitment to a negotiated settlement and accelerates progress. In South Africa's transition from 1990 to 1994, a clear pattern emerged. Initially, widespread political violence frustrated efforts to reach agreements and to implement peace accords. At one point, in mid-1992, the talks collapsed completely over allegations of state involvement in community-level violence. Toward the end of the process, however, major upsurges in violence did not impede progress because the parties themselves had recognized that the strife would not subside until the pacts leading to the celebrated April 1994 elections had been fully implemented. Despite major, last-hour, party-political faction fighting on the eve of the elections, the peace agreement was implemented and, over time, significant political violence has virtually disappeared from the South African scene, even as the country remains engulfed in post-settlement violence in a society that continues to be deeply divided by race, ethnicity, and inequality (du Toit 2001).

A STRATEGY FOR INTERVENTION

By expanding knowledge on the interplay between violence and progress in negotiation at various phases of conflict escalation and de-escalation, we may begin to identify the ways in which local and international conciliators and mediators can more effectively influence parties away from violence and toward negotiation. Armed with awareness of how violence affects talks, domestic or international third parties may be able to help create the structures and sequences of negotiations to make reaching and sustaining settlements more likely. As Donald Rothchild demonstrates in *Managing Ethnic Conflict in Africa* (1997), domestic conciliators in civil society and international mediators clearly create and organize incentives that strongly and regularly tip the balance toward cooperation in deeply rooted ethnic conflicts.

International mediators are involved now more than ever in mitigating the world's protracted ethnic disputes. They formulate the terms of agreement and, in some instances, help provide security guarantees through military and police cooperation. They send humanitarian relief and legions of relief workers. In the most extensive instances, the United Nations or other organizations have directly overseen implementation of peace agreements. International mediators have already begun to openly articulate that they anticipate violence and recognize the conclusion that peace processes must be able to withstand and absorb ongoing social violence. Ambassador Jacques Paul Klein, Special Representative of the Secretary General to Liberia, currently the UN's most extensive peace operation, remarked to the Security Council on September 16, 2003:

> For the past twelve years they have lived in hellish limbo, suffering at the whim of warlords and despots, exploited by a criminal kleptocracy without help or relief in sight. Their lives and their country are held hostage by armed drugged thugs who destroy the state and engulfed the region in chaos. It is hard to assess the psychological effects of these crimes against justice and humanity. . . . Life becomes cheap; nothing is absolutely safe or sure; deeds of injustice and violence

become common facts in daily life; and there is the ever-present fear of imminent war. Events, however revolting, are soon forgotten in our often tempo-centric world.

We [the UN] have an obligation to assist in putting an end to this cycle of brutality, violence, corruption and instability that has destroyed the social fabric of society and has also spilled over the borders of Liberia and profoundly affected the region. This effort will require dramatic, engaged and bold solutions.

RECOMMENDATIONS FOR POLICY AND PRACTICE

Recommendations for finding silver linings are never well accepted by those in the midst of a painful violent episode with loss of life, discouragement, and grieving. But perhaps by understanding when violence has in the past stimulated progress toward talks, analysis can help inform practice in anticipating when violence may occur, understanding the strategy of its perpetrators, and taking ameliorative measures to prevent, manage, and mitigate bloodshed in the future, such as the following:

ACTIVATE AND SUPPORT THE MODERATE, CENTRIST CORE. In deeply divided societies in the midst of a protracted search for peace, the lion's share of resources, diplomacy, and cooperation should be used to maintain and broaden the scope and strength of moderate, centrist elites within parties committed to negotiation. That is, can a sustainable centrist coalition formed by moderates be struck and maintained? In terms of anticipating violence, a central question emerges: How vulnerable are moderate elites favoring talks when an act of street violence induces a crisis that undermines public and elite support for the peace process? The ability of political leaders, who are ostensibly committed to talks, to persuade and/or control their own midlevel combatants is the most critical problem; after all, it is many of these midlevel functionaries who have the most to lose from peace and who appear to be most culpable for post-settlement violence.

EVALUATE INTRAPARTY DYNAMICS. It is also important to analyze the relationships between elites and midlevel elites in each party to the talks, and the relationships between them and the broader groups they purport to represent. Can elites, assuming they genuinely seek peace accords, carry their own organization's factions and their publics? Analyzing the relative strengths and weaknesses of the moderate coalition can also reveal the extent to which rejectionist violence will undermine moderates and exacerbate polarization to the point where talks are no longer sustainable.

ENVISION PROGRESS THROUGH IMPLEMENTATION. A third analytical and policy priority is to emphasize the stakes involved in progressing through negotiation. Many may seek to convince the parties to the conflict of the stakes involved if efforts to manage the conflict *fail* to progress. That is, the stakes are defined as a return to a bloody past that, against the odds, the parties have begun to escape. How high are the stakes if the bloody encounters of the past occur once again? Third-party intervenors can help reframe the stakes to ensure that the achievement of progress in talks will be mutually beneficial and that failure to progress will precipitate a zero-sum or even lose-lose situation. Stakes and attitudes in ethnic conflicts are related: when the stakes are so high that group elimination or subjugation is a real possibility, attitudes will remain essentialist—adversaries are to be beaten—rather than pragmatic. Attitudes are slow to change in ethnic conflicts such as those considered here, but the high stakes of violence may be enough to temper attitudes toward a "cold" cooperation.

MANAGE UNCERTAINTY. The extent to which intervention efforts are targeted at reducing uncertainty—for example, by seeking to put in place international confidence-building measures such as deployment of an observer mission—the greater the likelihood of bolstering the talks and preventing a recurrence of violence. Would-be conflict ameliorators may also amend the stakes by reframing the issue in non-zero-sum terms, for example, by exploring specific power-sharing options with the parties, such as creating an interim national unity or consensus-oriented government, and wielding leverage to induce them into such a pact. They may also buttress the commitment to continue negotiating with sweeteners, such as aid or recognition (a form of bestowing legitimacy) to change the payoff structure.

If the parties *are* fundamentally motivated to avoid the abyss from which they are trying to escape, third-party efforts may help prevent a recurrence of widespread violence. Intervention has a chance if it is institutionalized in the form of ongoing peacekeeping, monitoring, and observation and if it is pursued by accepted, eminent, high-level envoys drawing their clout from close coordination with pivotal states or the UN (Stedman, Rothchild, and Cousens 2002). The strategy of such assertive intervention should be aimed at reinforcing the basic belief of moderate elites that the risks of a negotiated settlement are preferable to the consequences of a return to war, as well as reinforcing a civil society that can transcend previous lines of conflict.

Parties in protracted peace processes must be encouraged, even admonished, to negotiate their way *through* the violence, to make progress not just in spite of violence that will likely occur but because of the continued violence itself. Failure to progress leaves the peace process hostage to those who prefer violence because their own interests are not furthered by the forging and implementation of a settlement, no matter how fair and creative it may appear as a resolution of the underlying problems in conflict. Finding the silver lining in violent crises involves seizing on a single idea: the continued progression of the peace process itself is the answer to ending violence over the long term.

The search for silver linings in violent confrontations is an elusive and seldom rewarding task; more often than not, violence undermines the pursuit of peace by reinforcing strategies and perceptions that encourage conflict. Problems of incoherence and uncertainty give powerful reasons for some protagonists to foment violence with the determined and strategic intent of inducing failure in the talks. This was the case in Rwanda in 1994 and is currently the case in many other peace processes. Today, demands by protagonists in conflicts from Russia to Israel to Colombia are similar: all violence must stop before negotiations can progress; there can be no talks while the war wages or while street-level clashes ensue. Such demands are inherently unrealistic and unachievable because they are at odds with the essential logic and incentive structure of violence. The imperatives for today's protracted peace processes are clear: violence should be anticipated and may well escalate while the talks occur; the centrist core must be able to negotiate through the violence and organize itself into a coherent state; and the implementation process should be vigorously pursued into the indefinite future with the expectation that, over time, post-settlement violence will eventually wither away.

ACKNOWLEDGMENTS

The research on which this paper is based was supported by the Norwegian Nobel Institute and a generous grant from the John D. and Catherine T. MacArthur Foundation. The author thanks John Darby, Dominic Murray, Donald Rothchild, Kristine Höglund, and the participants in Notre Dame's RIREC project for their insightful comments on earlier drafts of this paper.

NOTES

1. For the full story on the Arusha Agreement's collapse and the causes and precipitants of the Rwandan genocide, see Suhrke and Adelman (1999). The full text of the failed Arusha Agreement can be found at http://www.incore.ulst.ac.uk/cds/agreements/pdf/rwan1.pdf.

2. An exemplary situation is described by Steven R. Weisman in "Mideast Violence Threatens 'Quartet' Plan," *New York Times*, September 10, 2003.

3. For a similar finding, see also Marshall and Gurr (2003).

4. Schelling defines the *strategy* of conflict as the "interdependence of the adversaries' decisions and of the expectation of each others' behavior" (1966, 17). In essence, they adopt rational strategies to advance their aims, and the choice to talk or to fight is one such decision. According to Schelling, "The best

course of action for each participant depends on what he expects the other participants to do," with the knowledge that the other participants are making similar calculations with similar information (1966, 9–10).

5. In conventional international conflicts, this phenomenon has also been witnessed. For example, prior to the convening of the Paris peace talks to end the Vietnam War, military engagements (including aerial bombings by the United States), escalated sharply (Pillar 1983).

6. Bacharach and Lawler argue that "punitive tactics essentially attempt to force the opponent to make additional concessions beyond those that can be exacted by [ordinary] tactical concessions" (1981, 105).

7. This focus on intragroup differences builds on our understanding of the role of ethnic "outbidders" in exacerbating intergroup conflicts. See Rabushka and Shepsle (1972) and Horowitz (1985).

8. On the concept of turning points, see Druckman (1986). Because not all peace processes yield peace, it is clear that such turning points can be toward violence as well as away from it. Roy Licklider writes that "rather than a single pattern whereby civil violence is ended, it seems more useful to conceive of the termination of civil violence as a set of processes at which there are critical choice points. Selections at these points form alternative strategies of conflict termination" (1993, 18).

9. In an earlier study of the South African peace process from a democratization perspective, I showed preliminarily how at times political violence actually stimulated progress in talks (Sisk 1995, 217–20). This study will build on this earlier research with an in-depth analysis of more data and interviews that are specifically focused on this research problem.

10. Analyzing peace processes in terms of phases does not mean that for any given conflict situation a phase cannot be skipped, or that phases cannot overlap, or that the issues normally entertained at a very early stage of the process in one case may be those found at a later stage in another. See Zartman (1989a).

11. On formal theories of strategic choice, see Ordeshook (1989).

12. For retrospective analysis on the referendum as the war's trigger, see the Organization of Security and Cooperation in Europe report, http://www.csce.gov/pdf.cfm?file=1992ReferendumBH.pdf&pdf_id=134.

13. See Druckman (1986) for an attempt to quantify the concept (through indices) in the Philippines.

14. On the opening of formal negotiations in war termination, see Pillar (1983, 44–64).

15. On conciliation as a counterterrorist strategy, see Sederberg (1995).

16. See Reilly and Reynolds (2000) for a discussion of the linkages between electoral systems and conflict resolution.

17. "Progress" in negotiation is defined as the initiation of structured or formal talks following a period of prenegotiation, their sustainability in the face of challenge or opposition (especially violent opposition) during the uncertain interregnum, the clinching of a settlement (interim or final), and successful implementation.

18. See Bacharach and Lawler (1981, 179–203) for a fuller treatment of this theme.

JOHN DARBY

Post-Accord Violence
in a Changing World

All peace processes are played out to a ubiquitous soundtrack of violence. It helps to determine both their substance and approach and shift direction as processes move through their different phases. If opponents reach a peace agreement, violence continues as a major influence on postwar reconstruction. In Israel-Palestine, Guatemala, and elsewhere, casualty rates continued to be high after peace agreements had been signed. The effects fell unevenly across societies, as they had during the war. More civilians than militants were killed. The poor suffered more than the rich. The killings poisoned relationships as well as public attitudes toward the agreement, precisely because an agreement existed. People expect casualties during wars. They expect them to end when wars end. They never do.

An almost universal assumption in the literature on peacemaking is that peace processes are ipso facto desirable, and violence ipso facto an unpalatable and negative reality. Unpalatable certainly, but the chapters in this book illustrate that violence can, if managed strategically, accelerate progress toward a just and sustainable peace.

This concluding chapter reviews what we know about violence during the post-accord period. The discussion will be informed by and incorporate ideas from the other chapters, following the framework described in chapter 1: violence by the state, violence by militants, and violence in the community. It will also review how the postwar issues of demobilization, disarmament, and reintegration (DDR) and policing reform affect the implementation of peace agreements. The policy implications during each phase will be explored, including the potential for violence to advance as well as to obstruct a process—the potential silver lining described by Timothy Sisk. These themes will be discussed within the context of shifting patterns of violence globally, including the effects of the War against Terrorism on internal peace processes. How should this and other changes described in this book affect our thinking on peacemaking and conflict transformation? What changes can ensure that post-settlement euphoria is not followed by post-agreement *tristesse* and the all-important momentum is maintained?

VIOLENCE BY THE STATE

The use of force against internal violence is often regarded as a legitimate exercise of the state's responsibility to protect its citizens. Consequently, during intense conflicts and wars, the concerns of human rights activists focus on the illegitimate use of violence by the state, such as the abuse of the rules on arrest and detention, torture, and the use of unreasonable force, especially against civilians. When the war ends and a peace process begins, the water becomes more muddied. Illegal use of state violence to influence negotiations or to prepare for their collapse is often covert, always denied, and usually difficult to prove.

The achievement of an agreement removes the need for the glue that had united disparate elements within the government during negotiations. Implementation is an exasperating and lengthy business. Even politicians who negotiated the agreement may be expecting, and some may be working toward, its downfall. In this book Höglund and Zartman argue that three main elements associated with the state may be tempted to explore a conflict track: "the military, militias, and decision makers discontented with the turn to a settlement track." In Guatemala, for example, the sharp rise in crime that followed the 1996 peace accords were "often the work of members of the existing police force or the army," as well as unemployed ex-combatants.[1]

The emphasis by Höglund and Zartman on the role of militias in Congo-Brazzaville, Haiti, and elsewhere is both novel and timely. State actors opposed to an agreement may work in close association with militias to further their aims.

More frequently they are content to benefit covertly from militia activities. The violence in the Middle East following the Oslo Accords is characterized as one where Israeli government violence was countered by violence from Palestinian militias. The peculiar feature of militias, in their view, is that "they face all the mission-related temptations of the army, with no guaranteed role after settlement. Their irregularity, assured under conflict, has no cover under peace." As they are unlikely to have featured in the settlement, they continue to be potentially destabilizing elements in many post-accord settings.

One of the state's post-accord dilemmas is how to demonstrate its commitment to the settlement through demilitarization while retaining the ability to deal with militant groups and to reactivate its security machinery if the process collapses. Even if militants acknowledge this, however, they will also be reluctant to reduce their own capacity until the agreement has been implemented. This dilemma can best be resolved by a coordinated and phased approach to dismantling the military apparatus of both security forces and militants. Until the time comes when the army and police can be persuaded that downsizing offers opportunities as well as dangers, certain transitional procedures are possible. Governments can withdraw troops to barracks as an initial step toward troop reduction. They can incrementally replace the army with a reformed police force for security duties, as was done in South Africa and Israel-Palestine, or reduce security road checks in a manner similar to that used in Northern Ireland. Joint police-army patrols can be a useful tool in the transition to normal civilian policing. So can visible symbolic changes—the replacement of helmets with berets, different uniforms or regalia, less obtrusive security furniture, unarmed patrols, the opening of roads. Carefully choreographed transitions can reassure both the government's opponents and the general public without impairing public security in the event of a return to war. Such measures, however phased, are not carried out in a vacuum. Confidence is more likely to grow if agreement to demobilize the military is choreographed through carefully agreed upon steps and in parallel with disarmament by militants.

Who is to police the behavior of state actors during periods of reconstruction? International organizations usually work on the assumption that the state and its agencies, however corrupt and partial, have the prime responsibility to maintain law, order, and governance. But the state is also a primary actor in the conflict. It controls the greatest number of armed personnel and most of the weaponry, as well as the official agencies responsible for information and propaganda. So how are abuses by the state and by state personnel and agencies to be monitored and countered?

If a government abuses its power by continuing to use illegal violence after a peace agreement, as happened in Serbia-Montenegro, the principal onus for monitoring state behavior falls on agencies operating wholly or primarily outside the state. Human rights NGOs and international election monitoring played an important role in South Africa and in peace processes throughout Latin America. One of the strongest guarantees against the abuse of state power is a vigilant press. Attempts by the state to control the media in Burma and Zimbabwe eventually became one of the main issues in the conflict itself. The peace processes in Israel and Northern Ireland were played out in the full view of the world media, helping to ensure that any violence by individual members of the security forces or police was the subject of proper scrutiny.

Nicole Bell has described the difficulties inherent in the demobilization and reintegration of soldiers and pointed out the need for "additional longer-term investigation of beneficiaries and detailed cost analysis" and for donor agencies to establish a coordinated framework.[2] Frustration among members of the security forces, for example, can be a potential threat to any peace process. High among the causes of frustration is apprehension that their jobs are at risk. Unless steps are taken to ease their return to civilian life, dissatisfied and well-armed members of the security forces constitute as serious a threat to stability as their paramilitary counterparts.

THE THREAT FROM MILITANTS

The threat of violence by militants and ex-militants has been dominated by a debate on spoilers,[3] defined by Stedman as "leaders and parties who believe that peace emerging from negotiations threaten their power, worldview, and interests, and use violence to undermine attempts to achieve it" (Stedman 1997, 95). He describes three types of spoilers: total spoilers, whose goals are immutable and who "see the world in all-or-nothing terms"; limited spoilers, who have specific goals that may or may not be negotiable; and greedy spoilers, whose goals "expand or contract based on calculations of cost and risk" (Stedman 1997, 10–11).

A modification of Stedman's typology is used in this chapter in order to embrace all militants and ex-militants whose violence may threaten a peace process, including those who are engaged in negotiations and criminals who may undermine it unintentionally through their violent activities. The main threats come from four sources designated as *Dealers* (those who are prepared to negotiate); *Zealots* (those whose goal is to spoil the process by bringing it down through violence); *Opportunists* (those who may be persuadable under some circumstances to end violence); and *Mavericks* (those whose violence is primarily motivated by personal rather than political objectives).[4] The Zealots and Opportunists incorporate the three types of spoilers—total, limited, and greedy spoilers—described in Stedman's typology.

If peace processes are to survive the different forms of violence undermining them, different policy approaches are required toward these different interests. The key actors in any peace process are the Dealers, whose decision to negotiate initiated the process and without whose involvement the process ends. The key policy objective, it follows, is to ensure that they remain in the process. Their involvement as fully engaged partners is essential in order to negotiate and implement a peace agreement. Opportunists and Zealots are not always easy to distinguish. Both are usually smaller and more extreme groups that have been excluded from, or excluded themselves from, the process. The essential difference is that Opportunists may ultimately be open to participating in the process, while Zealots are likely to remain dedicated to its failure. The dilemma, then, is how to keep the door open for Opportunists while isolating the Zealots. If this is accomplished, the process must find a way of dealing with them, as well as with any Mavericks who also continue to use violence. One measure of success is the degree to which violence can be criminalized by dealing with it through the courts. This becomes more feasible if the Dealers feel sufficiently strong to condemn violence. Dealers never find this easy, as it allows Zealots to charge them with betrayal and to present themselves as the true patriots. Timing is crucial. In Northern Ireland the universal fury at the Omagh bombing in August 1998, and the marginalization of the bombers, allowed Sinn Féin to condemn a republican bomb for the first time. However, the strength of Hamas and the Islamic Zealots in Israel-Palestine prevented Arafat from such an unqualified condemnation, only allowing him to denounce its leader Sheik Yassin for "supporting terrorist activities,"[5]

Although these different groups require different approaches, there is sometimes a conspiracy to fudge the distinction between violence from parties outside the process and violence from those inside it. In order to keep the process on track, some violence associated with the Dealers may be ignored, or even defended, as long as it is not politically motivated. Thus the secretary of state for Northern Ireland, while condemning violence by zealots, was forced to rule that an IRA murder of a drug dealer did not breach the ceasefire; to rule otherwise would have meant expulsion of Sinn Féin at a sensitive stage of the process. Such realpolitik carries a price. It may encourage militant elements within the Dealer groups to test further the limits of tolerance, it provides ammunition for political opponents of the process, and it embarrasses supporters of the agreement.

Marie-Joëlle Zahar has returned to Albert Hirschman's 1970 book, *Exit, Voice and Loyalty*, to find a broader, more inclusive understanding of violence. She demonstrates that violence is a strategy used by actors seeking both voice (inclusion in or renegotiation of the peace agreement) and exit (disruption of peace). She outlines an analytical framework to develop better predictive and effective tools for the management of violence. There are two key factors in this framework: "capability, or the resources available to the groups and individuals to this end; and opportunity, or the constraints on violence posed by the presence and commitment of foreign interveners and by the commitment of other actors to the peace process." The main thrust of Zahar's argument is the need for a more analytical approach to the conditions and dynamics that determine the motives and actions of spoilers.

ON THE GROUND

Mary Kaldor (1999) has drawn attention to the recent emergence of "new wars" involving armed networks of nonstate and state actors. Among these actors are paramilitary groups, warlords, terrorist cells, fanatic volunteers, and units of the security services, "as well as mercenaries and private military companies" (Kaldor 1999); they also include "organized criminal groups." Alongside this development, however, especially in societies where state control is strong, an increase in political violence may actually be accompanied by a decline in recorded conventional crime. Crime rates were low in the Basque Country and South Africa, for example, while political violence was at its height. During the years of Northern Ireland's Troubles the numbers of burglaries, assaults, and thefts were consistently lower than those in England and Wales (see Geary and Morrison 1992). The reasons are varied. Policing is dominated by security concerns. Many hostile areas are not patrolled, leading to an under-recording of crime statistics. Paramilitary organizations claim, and often exercise, the right to police the areas under their control. If an agreement is reached, these conditions may be reversed. Roger Mac Ginty reviews six environmental factors that contribute to a postwar crime wave: state weakness, a culture permissive to crime, the presence of former combatants and military weapons, the nature and scale of development aid, and uneven economic development. "The link between these factors and crime is not automatic," Mac Ginty points out, "although each has the capacity to significantly enhance an environment conducive to crime."

The rise in crime is never easy to measure. "While many societies have experienced a dramatic increase in criminal violence after the signing of a peace agreement," Höglund and Zartman observe in this book, "it is often difficult to distinguish to what extent this is a continuation of violent practices from the war or a new phenomenon." Mac Ginty points out the obstacles to classifying and measuring postwar violence. These include a greater postwar willingness to report crime and a tendency to exaggerate it as the edges between political violence and conventional crime overlap. He describes this as "para-political crime."

Mac Ginty's careful unraveling of the key areas where military and conventional crime overlap, and the factors conducive to a rise in postwar crime, is a valuable advance toward a more nuanced approach to the problem. He argues that uneven economic development in postwar societies that are predominantly poor is a key explanation of growing crime.

A significant rise in post-accord crime is clearly a matter for concern, but does it necessarily pose a threat to the agreement itself? Mac Ginty's judgment is that crime has not been identified as the major factor contributing to the outright failure of a peace accord, but it can erode confidence in the agreement among the general population. As the sapping of unionist support for the Good Friday Agreement in Northern Ireland demonstrates, the accord may survive but be replaced only by an unstable and uncertain stasis. There are two more specific dangers: first, an authoritarian reaction to crime from the government may undermine "the liberalizing intentions and provisions of a peace accord"; and second, the evolution of vigilantism, a postwar problem deserving greater attention. In Guatemala vigilantes were responsible for killing dozens of suspected criminals in the six months after the accords; more than twenty lynchings followed in 1997.[6] Punishment beatings and shootings by paramilitary groups in Northern Ireland have been persistent drag anchors to post-accord reconciliation and reconstruction. Some of the worst violence in South Africa was caused by PAGAD (People Against Gangsterism and Drugs), who engaged in tit-for-tat killings with criminal gangs as well as in no-warning restaurant bombs. PAGAD was responsible for twenty bombings around Cape Town, including eight in 2000, leading the minister of justice to step up protection for judges and prosecutors involved in cases against PAGAD and to consider a ban. PAGAD's response was to threaten "one prosecutor, one bullet," a play on the radical mantra "one settler, one bullet" used during the anti-apartheid war.[7]

DEMOBILIZATION, DISARMAMENT, AND REINTEGRATION (DDR) AND POLICING

All peace processes give birth to a number of issues that were unthinkable while the fighting continued. How best to phase in the confidence-building measures demanded by both sides? Should amnesties or the early release of prisoners be introduced at an early stage as confidence-building gestures for paramilitaries? Should arms decommissioning be a precondition in order to reassure constitutional politicians? These issues, among them demobilization, disarmament, and reintegration (DDR), and reform of the police, are the stuff of post-accord politics. The agreement may sketch out general parameters of how they should be approached, but the fine details and implementation—what du Toit has called post-settlement settlements—form the new agenda for dispute (du Toit 2003).

While it is possible to identify general comparative tendencies in tackling post-accord problems, over-generalization is dangerous. The disarmament of para-militaries illustrates the point. The 1991 South African National Peace Accord did not ask the ANC to disband paramilitary units or hand over its arms caches; it required only that firearms not be displayed at public meetings. In Northern Ireland the demand for IRA decommissioning by unionists, and the IRA's tardi-ness in accepting it, was perhaps the most serious post-accord problem there. In this book Virginia Gamba passes somber judgment on recent approaches to DDR throughout the world: "Key objectives of a peace process are to secure peace, ensure demobilization, ensure disarmament, and assist in post-conflict recon-struction and development. If these objectives are not realized, peace cannot be consolidated. Since 1989 almost all cases of multinational peace-making and peace support operations have not fully realized the above-mentioned objectives." These failures were largely caused either by inability to establish postwar security or by problems of coordination between actors involved in post-conflict recon-struction during the transition from war to stability. Many of the worst failures highlighted by Gamba were in Africa, so it is ironic that Africa may be provid-ing a model for other continents and regions through the New Partnership for Africa's Development (NEPAD). Perhaps NEPAD's most important lesson is its willingness to provide reassurance for post-accord states by sketching in broad DDR objectives but having the confidence to leave the substance for later devel-opment. In Gamba's words, "the key to success on the ownership formula that lead to the signature in Lusaka was that NEPAD was not presented as a hard and fast plan but as a hard and fast idea." Most of all, it provided a mechanism for coor-dination not only between different functions (demobilization, disarmament, and reintegration) but also between the neighboring countries in the region.

Post-accord policing can be an equally difficult and contentious matter. The integration of ex-militants into the security system can be a two-edged sword. It removes potentially disruptive soldiers and weapons from the street, it legit-imizes irregular policing activities, and it provides additional police when they are most needed to deal with increased transitional violence. It certainly eased the transition in South Africa. By 1996, 16,000 former guerrillas had been absorbed into the South African army. However, when the Palestinian Liberation Organization (PLO) assumed responsibility for policing the Palestinian territories, it found itself in direct confrontation with Hamas and other Palestinian militant groups. If it is not possible to integrate ex-militants, reform of the existing police force becomes a priority task in a peace process. This process can sometimes be validated by the involvement of friendly external agents, as when the Spanish Civil Guards assisted in restructuring and retraining Guatemala's police.

Dominic Murray, in this volume, points out the peculiar problems of post-accord policing: "The emerging police force, therefore, will now be tackling criminals who in the past may have acted as protectors of, and were protected by, the communities of which they form part. . . . In addition, the steps necessary to restore some form of normality (searches, curfews, check points, etc.) are exactly those most likely to engender antagonism."

How is this problem to be tackled? By providing a sense of ownership, transparency, and accessibility through new police structures. This is easier said than done. Murray draws attention to the obstacles facing the creation of a more inclusive police force following a peace agreement: the introduction of community policing in a divided community; the acceptance of paramilitaries as police officers; the risk of institutionalizing segregation. The police are likely to be "reluctant reformers," so change is unlikely to be achieved rapidly.

Reciprocation and coordination are the keys in approaching both DDR and policing reform. Changes in policing, whether through integration or reform, must be accompanied by a new approach to in-service and preservice training. Failure to demilitarize Northern Ireland's security apparatus while simultaneously decommissioning paramilitary weaponry seriously damaged the implementation of the Good Friday Agreement. In retrospect it is clear that elements in the ultimate agreement usually associated with post-accord disputes—policing reforms, reductions in the military power of all combatants—are less likely to obstruct reconstruction if they are addressed and publicized during the early stages of peace processes.

THE NEED TO DISAGGREGATE

The different threats from violence discussed in this book do not carry equal weight. They vary substantially between different peace processes. In Israel-Palestine violence from the Israeli state and violence from Palestinian militants were both responsible for the failure of the Oslo Accords; conventional crime was low, and DDR was not even under discussion. In South Africa and Guatemala, on the other hand, violent crime dominates the postwar scene, although a case might be made that so far it has not posed a threat to the agreements, except insofar as it undermines post-accord reconstruction.

To some degree each type of violence tends to surface during a different stage of a peace process, although there are considerable overlaps between them. Violence from both the state and from militants is particularly threatening during the early stages of peace processes, but the militant threat may persist throughout all phases. The rise of violence in the community, especially the rise in conventional crime, follows fast on the heels of the ending of political violence and may continue to grow after an agreement has been reached. DDR and reform of the police and army are implementation issues and usually follow peace agreements.

There are two good reasons why it is important to analyze the distinctions between different forms of post-accord violence. The first is that each form requires a different policy approach from all the actors in a peace process. The best safeguards against state violence, for example, are external monitors, such as international and regional organizations, nongovernmental groups, and a strong independent media reporting illegal actions to the outside world—a reality recognized by the attempts of some governments to exclude or control their access to scenes of violence. An awareness of the distinction between different forms of violence is even more necessary when dealing with militants because different types of spoilers require different treatments. Marie-Joëlle Zahar argues that it is essential to differentiate between inside and outside spoilers, and their position vis-à-vis the peace agreement, in order "to distinguish analytically between violence that seeks to secure voice and violence that expresses exit." Policy should reflect these distinctions. It should aim to support those ex-militants who have entered negotiations, to leave the door open for other militants to enter the process under strict conditions, and to apply the rule of law to isolate and sanction the zealots and mavericks who continue to use violence.

The second reason for distinguishing carefully between different forms of violence is that the appropriate policy for some of these problems may actually exacerbate others. For example, the most obvious approach to the rise in postwar crime described by Roger Mac Ginty is to increase police presence on the streets. But the police are unlikely to be universally regarded as impartial because of their racial or ethnic composition, heritage, and instincts. Consequently, it is possible, indeed probable, that a stronger police presence may not only provide targets for zealots but also lead to confrontations between police and activists, as has happened in the Basque Country and Northern Ireland.

VIOLENCE AS CATALYST FOR PEACE?

Alongside the many cases in which violence has demonstrated its ability to derail peace negotiations stands a body of atrocities that became catalysts for moving toward settlement. One was the Omagh bomb in Northern Ireland, planted by a splinter republican group within months of the 1998 Good Friday Agreement. The "Real" IRA bomb struck indiscriminately against both communities, killing twenty-nine people. It defied the popular support for the Good Friday Agreement in the recent referenda in both parts of Ireland. For the first time Sinn Féin's Gerry Adams condemned a republican bomb "without any equivocation whatsoever." His colleague Martin McGuinness went further: "We see our job to be one of stopping the activities of these people."[8] The Omagh bomb also provided the opportunity for both governments to harmonize and toughen their antiterrorist powers with virtually no opposition. This in turn allowed the unionist leader David Trimble, uncharacteristically, to compliment the government response in the Irish Republic. In effect Omagh licensed a number of actors who had intellectually accepted the need to make concessions to actually do so. In addition, public hostility to the Omagh bomb caused consternation among spoiler groups. Within four days of the bomb those responsible for planting it, the "Real" IRA, had declared a ceasefire. Three days later the Irish National Liberation Army (NLA), one of the most violent of the republican groups, followed suit with "a complete ceasefire." Violence, or rather spoiler violence, had become temporarily unfashionable.

Responses such as those following Omagh are dramatic, but not unique, in peace processes. Occasionally certain atrocities provoke universal condemnation and galvanize popular reaction against the perpetrators. The Basque Country and South Africa have experienced similar incidents.[9] Instead of destabilizing negotiations or an agreement, they became a stimulus for the negotiations (du Toit 2001).

What is the nature of these atrocities that converts them into catalysts for peace? Why did they have such a powerful effect when so many appalling actions from the past did not? It has been argued that three critical factors in making violence a catalyst for peace are quality of leadership, the cohesion of the groups in negotiation, and timing (Darby 2001, 97–99). If these factors are in place, the atrocities enable public outrage to be harnessed rather than simply vented. It is the harnessing that is important. Outrage without a mechanism to enforce it fades away, as earlier peace movements had faded away. A peace agreement creates a context for connecting anger to the political process.

The main obstacles to postwar violence producing positive results, as Timothy Sisk points out, are general uncertainty about outcomes, continuing ethnonationalist ideology, and the continuing use of violence by any negotiating party. In relation to post-accord violence, he poses the question, "can the crises that violent encounters produce spur the protagonists in conflict toward greater cooperation?" The likeliness of this happening depends on a range of factors, including a relative symmetry of power between, and cohesion within, the main parties. A more precise understanding of how violence influences post-accord reconstruction, as it affects every other stage in the process, provides guidelines for creating the right incentives to "tip the balance toward cooperation in deeply rooted ethnic conflicts."

CONSIDERATIONS AND APPROACHES

The principal message from all the chapters in this book is that violence is unavoidable both during peace negotiations and while a peace agreement is being implemented. Whether its effects are positive or negative depends on the ability of peacemakers to develop appropriate strategies in response to it. Successful postwar reconstruction requires leaders to think differently about violence and to adopt three levels of response: a strategic approach, an incentives-based approach, and a reciprocal approach.

A STRATEGIC APPROACH

At each stage during peace processes, and for each set of actors, the use of violence is primarily a matter of calculation rather than spontaneity. "In making decisions about the potential use of violence," Zahar contends, "militants and ex-militants assess the costs and benefits of each course of action." In Sisk's words, violence is "an integral part of the overall bargaining process in contemporary civil wars."

The resumption of violence can have either a positive or negative effect on postwar reconstruction. Sisk argues that sharp rises in the intensity of violence are invariably critical turning points in peace processes. They "force those at the negotiation table to make critical choices, essentially whether to recoil and return to the fight, or hunker down, continue talking, and weather the political storm." Höglund and Zartman also emphasize how violence forces decision makers "to consider the consequences of continued armed conflict (or fear of war) and the consequences of a negotiated settlement (or fear of peace)"; they conclude that a "strategic rethinking toward negotiation comes about when the two factors point the decision makers in the same direction."

Under what circumstances can these fears be utilized to drive peace negotiations forward? While the use of violence increases distrust and disillusionment among opponents and may drive them back to war, in different circumstances, as Höglund and Zartman point out, "it may also influence the opposing side's fears of continued conflict, making it more determined in its attempts to pursue peace. With this use, violence can directly accelerate negotiations and the implementation of a peace agreement. Indirectly, violence by the state and its allies can have a reverse effect by raising opposition to violence and influencing public opinion in favor of the peace process."

Sisk's conclusion that the central need is the management and reduction of uncertainty during negotiations and after agreements have been reached is echoed throughout the chapters in this book. He suggests a number of strategic requirements to reduce the negative effects of violence. These include the need to activate and support the moderate, centrist core; the need to evaluate intra-party dynamics, especially the relationships between elites and midlevel elites to ensure that leaders can carry their own supporters; and the need to envision progress through implementation, especially by reminding people of the cost of a return to violence. Zahar also argues that the spoiler debate needs to be reframed within a broader context with a "focus on the interplay between moti-vation and context."

AN INCENTIVES-BASED APPROACH

Successful reconstruction requires a combination of sanctions and rewards. Stedman and others have emphasized the importance of external custodians to consolidate peace agreements, but the allied use of incentives has received less attention. Each form of violence, at each stage in each peace process, needs to be separately identified, analyzed, and treated appropriately in order to gain better understanding of the factors that persuade different actors to reject violence. Sisk points out, for example, that "the cost-benefit calculations of further fight-ing may be markedly different for different parties depending on their level of devotion to the conflict." Within countries, he points out, "the electoral system is a key incentive structure that affects the propensity for rejectionists to foment violence. If a rejectionist party believes it can win a few seats in the new parlia-ment, rather than being completely excluded from the new system, this incen-tive may be enough to widen the base of the peace process and bring in those with the capacity to 'spoil.'"

Among the most effective incentives are examples of successful implemen-tation in other places. The best models for effective reconstruction are often, but not always, regional. In Guatemala and El Salvador, for example, approaches to policing reform borrowed heavily and often profitably on Latin American and Spanish models that might have less relevance for some other regions. In Europe, too, there was a symbiotic relationship between approaches to negotiations in Northern Ireland, the Basque Country, and Corsica.[10] Virginia Gamba has point-ed to the potential of the New Partnership for Africa's Development (NEPAD) to provide a framework and inspiration for regional DDR in Africa and raises the

question of the possibility of its application elsewhere. Negotiators are often willing to adapt approaches from other places. The use of sufficient consensus to deal
with the problem of multiple negotiators in South Africa is now commonplace in
peace processes. Northern Ireland's Mitchell Principles introduced a model for
attracting militants into negotiations while addressing the concerns of constitutional politicians. It only requires minor incentives to encourage a more systematic search for the most appropriate and promising models.

A RECIPROCAL APPROACH

Governments are often reluctant to begin the reduction of its security apparatus
without first testing the seriousness of their opponents. The suspicion is mutual. In this atmosphere, confidence-building measures—early release of political
prisoners, policing reform, DDR—may reassure ex-militants, but they are also
likely to create anxiety among one's own supporters and the community at large.
Unilateral confidence-building gestures are unlikely to succeed. Consequently,
concessions between the government and militants on issues of deep mutual
suspicion must be carefully choreographed.

The Pastrana peace initiative in Colombia highlights the dangers if demobilization, disarmament, and reintegration are not carefully managed. In
November 1998, shortly after Andres Pastrana became president, he took an exceptionally innovative gamble by declaring a large swath of southern Colombia a
demilitarized zone and handing control over to the most powerful militant organization, the Revolutionary Armed Forces of Colombia (FARC). No reciprocal concessions were required, not even a ceasefire. His aim was to persuade them of his
good intentions and to encourage them to join the negotiations. The experiment
failed. "By all accounts except their own, the rebels have abused the spirit of the
government's inducement by stockpiling weapons, recruiting and training new
fighters, killing perceived enemies and protecting lucrative drug operations."[11]
Despite this, Pastrana gambled again in April 2000 with the second largest militant group, the National Liberation Army (ELN). He agreed to pull troops and
police out of a northern region the size of Switzerland, but this time only in return for a national peace convention and after a "general framework of understanding" had been reached.

There is nothing new about adopting a reciprocal approach to concessions during peace negotiations. As early as 1962 Charles Osgood proposed the GRIT
(Graduated and Reciprocated Initiatives in Tension Reduction) approach, a phased
program of measures to achieve a downward spiral of violence. The GRIT approach
aimed to reduce risk for both sides by having them retain their retaliatory capabili-

ty." There is considerable laboratory support for this approach (Lindskold, 1978), and Pettigrew points to some success at the macro level in the Middle East and Northern Ireland:

> Several decades ago, Israel allowed Egypt to reopen the Suez Canal. Egypt reciprocated by allowing ships bound for Israel to use the canal. These acts reduced tension enough to make successful negotiations between the two nations possible. . . . Senator George Mitchell employed a version of GRIT in Northern Ireland and recommended it for defusing the Middle Eastern conflict. But this strategy cannot begin as long as each side demands the other make the first concessions. (Pettigrew 2002, 78)

As Tim Sisk points out, peace settlements "are package proposals that resolve multiple issues simultaneously by linking them." The package is often assembled toward the end of negotiations, after the components in the package have been negotiated separately, often by separate teams. Interim announcements about partial agreements run the risk of undermining a comprehensive settlement by subjecting it to premature scrutiny while talks on other matters continue. However, there are strong arguments for deliberately linking together separate issues in dispute. It allows for greater flexibility in negotiation. It encourages the view that peace agreements are trade-off packages and thus builds public confidence. In particular, it demonstrates to one's supporters that sacrifices have been made by their opponents as well as by themselves. Some issues have particularly strong potential for linkages. They include early prisoner release and the effect of it on victims; demobilization and disarmament; and differing approaches to policing reform.

The early release of prisoners is characteristically one of the earliest demands from militants. Victims' grievances, including truth commissions, are usually addressed much later, during the implementation of peace accords. The release of prisoners can help build confidence during the early suspicions of a peace process, but it also reminds the relatives and friends of their victims—police, soldiers, security staff and, most of all, civilians—of the losses they have suffered during the fighting. At its most emotive level this includes the problem of the disappeared, when family members are still ignorant of where the bodies of victims have been disposed. Early releases of prisoners, therefore, are likely to be more tolerable if they are accompanied by recognition of and compensation for the harm done to the bereaved and the wounded. This raises a problem of sequencing. In policy terms the sensitive issue of victims' compensation should be addressed during negotiations rather than post-settlement, not only for reasons of equity but because public outrage may turn parts of society against the peace process itself, as evidenced in Israel and Northern Ireland. The reciprocation between disarmament of militants and demobilization of security forces is more obvious. It is natural for combatants to want to test their opponents' sincerity before disarming themselves, which can bring a peace process to a stalemate. Consequently, there is need to orchestrate reciprocal concessions on demilitarization and decommissioning during peace negotiations and to do this very early in the proceedings. A similar situation exists with respect to the reform of policing. Whether ex-militants are integrated into the police force or the force is reformed internally, early implementation is also likely to enhance the chances of successful policing and security reform.

Reciprocation requires concessions from both the government and its opponents. The ending of a war leaves a residue of lawlessness that sits uneasily in the no man's land between political violence and crime. Militant organizations are often reluctant to abandon the power and policing functions they had previously exercised, and violence may continue in the form of punishment beatings and killings, criminal activities, and vigilante attacks against the criminal activities of others. During negotiations what ought to be unacceptable is accepted as necessary to achieve the greater good of a peace agreement. Uneasy distinctions are made between political violence that breaks the ceasefire and other forms of violence that do not. It is essential to build into the agreement the recognition that such violence will seriously undermine postwar reconstruction and that continuing ambivalence toward it will not be tolerated. If the discussion is deferred until implementation starts, the advantages of reciprocity may be lost.

CHANGING CONTEXTS:
THE END OF THE PEACE PROCESS?

Violence from within may threaten any peace process, but the regional and global contexts may also have a powerful effect on whether conflicts move toward violence or settlement. The context alters continually. During the Cold War the two superpowers maintained their own form of order against threats of violence from within their own areas of control. The Soviet Union stepped in forcibly when it felt its interests were threatened by liberation movements in Hungary, Yugoslavia, and Russia. The United States maintained a similar control in the Americas.

The collapse of the Soviet Union effectively ended the superpower system. The successor states reflected old national and ethnic allegiances, and some of them also inherited discontented national and ethnic minorities. Mary Kaldor (1999) and others have argued that the challenges to state autonomy and author-

ity internationally have led to a succession of "new wars," in which the traditional state monopoly on the use of violence was increasingly undermined. The distinctions between traditional wars, international crime, and human rights violations became increasingly blurred. However, these developments were paralleled
by the new approaches to peacemaking in South Africa and elsewhere that
emerged during the 1990s. These approaches, described in this book, were characterized by peace processes that evolved primarily through internal negotiations, with the United Nations and external actors often playing subsidiary roles.

Developments following the events of September 11, 2001, have again altered
the global context for many traditional conflicts. Terrorism has been elevated
from the local to the international stage. President Bush's declaration of a War
against Terrorism had a number of local and regional consequences. Not least of
these is the use of the word "terrorism" itself. Prior to the 9/11 attacks, academics
tiptoed around the word, wary of its lack of precision and its pejorative connotations. They were aware that wars won by terrorists, including those in North
America in the 1770s and throughout Africa and Asia in the 1950s and 1960s,
are often acknowledged retrospectively as wars of liberation. Since the 9/11
attacks the use of the word has become commonplace, not only in the media and
everyday speech but increasingly in the academic literature on international and
internal violence. It has not lost its imprecise or pejorative connotations.

The War against Terrorism was declared globally but fought locally. It has
become more difficult to distinguish between the war against al-Qaida and longstanding guerrilla struggles in Indonesia, Palestine, and Sudan. The effects of this
conflation between terrorism and civil wars have been critical, both for governments and for militants opposing them. Some governments, encouraged by the
growing concern about terrorism, have distanced themselves from the possibility of negotiations with militant minorities in their own countries. Others
have justified tougher security approaches as part of the War against Terrorism.
Actions such as torture of prisoners and assassinations of militant leaders, previously conducted covertly by governments in the interests of security, are likely to
be carried out more openly, encouraged by the new atmosphere of antiterrorism.

The effects of these changes on militant opponents of a government have
been two-fold. The stronger actions have angered many Muslim groups. Violent
resistance has intensified, especially in parts of Asia and the Middle East. On the
other hand, it is clear that the new global temperature has reduced support from
diaspora populations for the Tamil Tigers in Sri Lanka, for dissident republican
groups in Ireland, and elsewhere. Military intervention by governments is applying pressure on their campaigns. Paradoxically, the War against Terrorism provided a potential international safety net for governments to engage in a peace process
with dissidents. If militants call off talks and restart the war—and the sanctions

against this have increased—the international community seems ready to provide substantial assistance to governments. One might argue about the relative benefits and costs. What is indisputable is that the War against Terrorism has significantly altered the local climate within which ethnic conflicts are conducted.

Even before the 9/11 attacks, a view was growing that the optimism for peace processes during the 1990s has not been justified by subsequent developments. Part of the gloom arose from the erosion of peace after so many agreements had been reached. Edward Said entitled his 2000 collection of essays on the Middle East *The End of the Peace Process*. Since then, the model of peace processes developed during the 1990s has been further undermined by the War against Terrorism and the responses to it. This model was dominated by an inclusive approach to peacemaking, one that sought opportunities for negotiation rather than confrontation; its characteristics were compromise and optimism. The War against Terrorism has encouraged an alternative model, one that sees the possibility of victory over dissent; its characteristics are strength and the presentation of stark choices. The two models coexist.

The question is, Are we moving toward a form of peacemaking that is predominantly driven by security interests rather than by opportunities for a negotiated settlement? Is this a temporary phenomenon, or a sea change?

NOTES

1. *Economist*, June 28, 1997, 14.

2. See Ball (1997). Kumar's book (1997) provides a fine overview of postwar reconstruction.

3. For a fuller description of spoiler violence, see Stedman (1997).

4. See Darby (2001) for a development of this analysis.

5. *Jordan Times*, November 2, 1998.

6. *Economist*, June 28, 1997.

7. *New York Times*, September 9, 2000.

8. *Observer* (London), August 6, 1998.

9. For further discussion of catalytic violence, see Darby (2001, 95–100).

10. For a more detailed discussion of how negotiators actively seek models, see Darby and Mac Ginty (2003, 245–55).

11. Larry Rohter, "Columbia Talks Threatened," *New York Times*, September 25, 1999.

Bibliography

ACCORD. 1998. "Safeguarding Peace: Cambodia's Constitutional Challenge." In *ACCORD: An International Review of Peace Initiatives 5*. London: Conciliation Resources.

Atlas, Pierre M., and Roy Licklider. 1999. "Conflict Among Former Allies after Civil War Settlement: Sudan, Zimbabwe, Chad, and Lebanon." *Journal of Peace Research* 36 (1): 35–54

Azar, E., et al. 1978. "Protracted Social Conflict: Theory and Practice in the Middle East." *Journal of Palestine Studies* 8 (1): 41–60.

——. 1990. *The Management of Protracted Social Conflict: Theory and Cases.* Aldershot: Dartmouth.

Babovic, B. 2002. *On Police Reform in the Federal Republic of Yugoslavia and Serbia.* Working Paper Series no. 10. Geneva: Geneva Centre for the Democratic Control of Armed Forces (DCAF).

Bacharach, Samuel B., and Edward J. Lawler. 1981. *Bargaining: Power, Tactics and Outcomes.* San Francisco: Jossey-Bass.

Ball, Nicole. 1996. "The Challenge of Rebuilding War-Torn Societies." In *Managing Global Chaos: Sources of and Responses to International Conflict*, ed. Chester A. Crocker, Fen Osler Hampson, and Pamela Aall (pp. 607–22). Washington, D.C.: United States Institute of Peace Press.

——. 1997. "Demobilizing and Reintegrating Soldiers: Lessons from Africa." In *Rebuilding Societies after Civil Wars*, ed. Krishna Kumar (pp. 85–106). Boulder, Colo.: Lynne Rienner.

Bardon, J. 1992. *A History of Ulster.* Belfast: Blackstaff Press.

Barry, Brian. 1991. *Democracy and Power: Essays in Political Theory.* Oxford: Clarendon Press.

Bayley, D. H. 1997. "The Contemporary Practices of Policing: A Comparative View." In *National Institute of Justice Series, Civilian Police and Multinational Peacekeeping.* Washington, D.C.: Department of Justice.

Berdal, Mats, and David M. Malone, eds. 2000. *Greed and Grievance: Economic Agendas in Civil Wars.* Boulder, Colo.: Lynne Rienner, and Ottawa: International Development Research Centre.

Boothby, D. 1998. *The UNTAES Experience: Weapons Buy-backs in Eastern Slovonia, Baranja and Western Sirmium (Croatia), Report 12.* Bonn: Bonn International Center for Conversion.

Brahimi, L. 2000. *Report on the Panel on United Nations Peace Operations.* New York: United Nations.

Brown, Michael, E., et al., eds. 1997. *Nationalism and Ethnic Conflict.* Cambridge, Mass.: MIT Press.

Call, Charles. 1999. "Crime and Peace: Successful Peace Processes Produce the World's Most Violent Countries." Paper presented at the Annual Conference of the International Studies Association, Washington D.C.

Call, Charles, and William Stanley. 2002. "Civilian Security." In *Ending Civil Wars: The Implementation of Peace Agreements,* ed. by Stephen Stedman, Donald Rothchild, and Elizabeth Cousens (pp. 303–26). Boulder, Colo.: Lynne Rienner.

Cannings, Kathleen. 1992. "The Voice of the Loyal Manager: Distinguishing Attachment from Commitment." *Employee Responsibilities and Rights Journal* 5 (3): 36–64.

Cilliers, J., and Dietrich C. 2000. *Angola's War Economy: The Role of Oil and Diamonds.* Pretoria, South Africa: Institute for Security Studies.

Collier, Paul. 2000. "Rebellion as a Quasi-Criminal Activity." *Journal of Conflict Resolution* 44 (December): 839–53.

——. 2003. *Breaking the Conflict Trap: Civil War and Development Policy.* Washington, D.C.: World Bank.

Collier, Paul, and Anne Hoeffler. 2001. *Greed and Grievance in Civil Wars.* Washington D.C.: World Bank.

Committee on the Administration of Justice. 1999. *The Agreement and a New Beginning to Policing in Northern Ireland.* Conference Report. Belfast: Committee on the Administration of Justice.

Constantine, T. 2001. *Report of the Independent Commission on Policing for Northern Ireland.* Belfast: Northern Ireland Office.

Covic, N. 2001. Address to the United Nations Security Council, September 27, 2001. Available online at www.serbia.gov.yu.

Cramphorn, C. 2001. "Human Rights and Police Accountability." Paper presented at Human Rights and Policing Conference, Belfast.

Crampton, R. J. 2002. *The Balkans Since the Second World War.* London: Longman.

Crawshaw, R. 1999. *Police Composition and Training in the Agreement and a New Beginning to Policing in Northern Ireland.* Belfast: Committee on the Administration of Justice.

Crocker, Chester A. 1992. *High Noon in South Africa.* New York: W.W. Norton.

Crocker, Chester A., Fen Osler Hampson, and Pamela Aall, eds. 2001. *Turbulent Peace: The Challenges of Managing International Conflict.* Washington, D.C.: United States Institute of Peace Press.

Darby, John. 1995. *What's Wrong with Conflict?* Occasional Paper. Coleraine: Centre for the Study of Conflict, University of Ulster.

——. 1997. *Scorpions in a Bottle: Conflicting Cultures in Northern Ireland.* London: Minority Groups Press.

——. 2000. "Violence and Peace Processes." In *Report,* the Joan B. Kroc Institute for International Peace Studies (pp. 13–18). Notre Dame, Ind.: University of Notre Dame.

———. 2001. *The Effects of Violence on Peace Processes.* Washington, D.C.: United States Institute of Peace Press.

Darby, John, and Roger Mac Ginty. 2000. *The Management of Peace Processes.* New York: St. Martin's.

———. 2002. *Guns and Government: The Management of the Northern Ireland Peace Process.* Basingstoke: Palgrave.

———, eds. 2003. *Contemporary Peacemaking: Conflict, Violence, and Peace Processes.* London and New York: Palgrave-Macmillan.

De Clerq, D. 1999. *Destroying Small Arms and Light Weapons: Survey of Methods and Practical Guide, Report 13.* Bonn: Bonn International Center for Conversion.

de Leon, Arévalo. 1998. *Sobre Arenas Movedizas: Sociedad, Estado y Ejército en Guatemala 1997.* Guatemala: FLASCO.

De Silva, K. M., and S. W. R. Samarasinghe, eds. 1993. *Peace Accords and Ethnic Conflict.* London and New York: Pinter.

De Soysa, I. 2002. "Paradise Is a Bazaar: Greed, Creed, and Governance in Civil War, 1989–1999." *Journal of Peace Research* 39 (4): 395–416.

Doyle, Michael, Ian Johnstone, and Robert Orr. 1997. *Keeping the Peace: Multidimensional UN Operations in Cambodia and El Salvador.* Cambridge: Cambridge University Press.

Druckman, Daniel. 1986. "Stages, Turning Points, and Crises." *Journal of Conflict Resolution* 30 (2): 327–60.

Duffy, Gavin, and Natalie Frensley. 1989. *Community Conflict Processes: Mobilization and Demobilization in Northern Ireland.* Working Paper no. 13. Syracuse: Syracuse University.

Dunn, S. 1995. *Facets of the Conflict in Northern Ireland.* London: Macmillan Press.

Du Toit, Pierre. 2001. *South Africa's Brittle Peace: The Problem of Post-Settlement Violence.* Basingstoke: Palgrave.

———. 2003. "Why Post-Settlement Settlements?" *Journal of Democracy* 14 (3): 104–18.

Edwards, A., and P. Gill. 2002. "The Politics of 'Transnational Organized Crime': Discourse, Reflexivity and the Narration of 'Threat.'" *British Journal of Politics and International Relations* 4 (2): 245–67.

Enderlin, Charles. 2002. *Le rêve brisé.* Paris: Fayard.

Farer, T. 1999. *Transnational Crime in the Americas.* New York: Routledge.

Fearon, James. 1998. "Commitment Problems and the Spread of Ethnic Conflict." In *The International Spread of Ethnic Conflict: Fear, Diffusion, and Escalation,* ed. David Lake and Donald Rothchild (pp. 107–26). Princeton, N.J.: Princeton University Press.

Fortna, Virginia Page. 2004. *Peace Time: Cease-Fire Agreements and the Durability of Peace.* Princeton, N.J.: Princeton University Press.

G8. 2003. *Implementation Report by Africa Personal Representatives to Leaders on the G8 Africa Action Plan.* Evian: G8 Summit.

Gamba, V. 2003. "Managing Violence: Disarmament and Demobilization." In *Contemporary Peacemaking: Conflict, Violence, and Peace Processes*, ed. John Darby and Roger MacGinty (pp. 125–36). London and New York: Palgrave-Macmillan.

Gastrow, Peter. 1995. *Bargaining for Peace: South Africa and the National Peace Accord.* Washington, D.C.: United States Institute for Peace.

Geary, R., and J. Morrison. 1992. "The Perception of Crime." In *Social Attitudes in Northern Ireland: The Second Report,* ed. P. Stringer and G. Robinson. Belfast: Blackstaff Press.

Geller, Daniel, and David Singer. 1998. *Nations at War: A Scientific Study of International Conflict.* New York: Cambridge University Press.

George, Alexander L. 1993. *Bridging the Gap: Theory and Practice in Foreign Policy.* Washington, D.C.: United States Institute of Peace Press.

———. 1994. "Theory and Practice." In *The Limits of Coercive Diplomacy,* ed. George E. Williams. Boulder, Colo.: Westview Press.

Glenny, M. 1999. *The Balkans, 1804–1999: Nationalism, War and the Great Powers.* London: Granta.

Gurr, Ted Robert. 2001. "Minorities and Nationalists: Managing Ethnopolitical Conflict in the New Century." In *Turbulent Peace: The Challenges of Managing International Conflict,* ed. Chester A. Crocker, Fen Osler Hampson, and Pamela Aall (pp. 163–88). Washington, D.C.: United States Institute of Peace Press.

Guelke, Adrian. 2000. "Interpretations of Political Violence during South Africa's Transition." *Politikon* 27 (2): 239–54.

Haass, Richard N. 1990. *Conflicts Unending: The United States and Regional Disputes.* New Haven, Conn.: Yale University Press.

———. 2002. "Reflections on U.S. Policy One Year On." Opening Speech at the IISS Global Strategic Review, September 13–15, London.

Hampson, Fen Osler. 1996. *Nurturing Peace: Why Peace Settlements Succeed or Fail.* Washington, D.C.: United States Institute of Peace Press.

Harnischfeger, J. 2003. "The Bakissi Boys: Fighting Crime in Nigeria." *Journal of Modern African Studies* 41 (1): 23–49.

Hartzell, Caroline, and Donald Rothchild. 1997. "Political Pacts as Negotiated Agreements: Comparing Ethnic and Non-Ethnic Cases." *International Negotiation* 2: 147–71.

Hewitt, Christopher. 1993. *Consequences of Political Violence.* Aldershot, England: Dartmouth Publishing.

Hirschman, Albert O. 1970. *Exit, Voice, and Loyalty: Responses to Decline in Firms, Organizations, and States.* Cambridge, Mass.: Harvard University Press.

———. 1974. "'Exit, Voice, and Loyalty': Further Reflections and a Survey of Recent Contributions." *Social Sciences Information* 13 (1): 1–26.

———. 1978. "Exit, Voice, and the State." *World Politics* 30: 90–107.

Holbrooke, Richard. 1999. *To End a War.* New York: Modern Library.

Höglund, Kristine. 2001. "Violence: Catalyst or Obstacle to Conflict Resolution? Seven Propositions Concerning the Effect of Violence on Peace Negotiations." Research Paper No. 3. University of Uppsala: Department of Peace and Conflict.

Holm, T. T., and E. B. Eide, eds. 2000. *Peace Building and Police Reform*. Portland, Ore.: Cass.

Horowitz, Donald. 1985. *Ethnic Groups in Conflict*. Berkeley: University of California Press.

Huntington, S. P. 1992. *The Third Wave: Democratization in the Late Twentieth Century*. Norman: University of Oklahoma Press.

International Crisis Group. 2001. *Bosnia's Precarious Economy: Still Not Open for Business*. Report 115. London: ICG.

Jacobs, D. 1979. "Inequality and Police Strength: Conflict Theory and Coercive Control in Metropolitan Areas." In *American Sociological Review* 44 (6): 913–25.

Kaldor, Mary. 1999. *New and Old Wars: Organised Violence in a Global Era*. Cambridge: Polity Press.

Kaufman, S. 2001. *Modern Hatreds: The Symbolic Politics of Ethnic War*. Ithaca, N.Y.: Cornell University Press.

Kecskemeti, Paul. 1970. "Political Rationality in Ending War. In *How Wars End*, ed. William T. R. Fox (pp. 105–15). Philadelphia: Annals of the American Academy of Political and Social Science.

Kelly, R. W. 1995. "American Law Enforcement Perspectives on Policing in Emerging Societies." Paper presented at Conference on Policing in Emerging Democracies, Washington, D.C.

Kesetovic, C. 2002. "Police Public Relations as a Function of Crime Prevention." Paper presented to the Conference on Policing in Central and Eastern Europe: Deviance, Violence and Victimization, Ljubljana.

King, Charles. 1997. *Ending Civil Wars*. Adelphi Paper 308. London: International Institute for Strategic Studies.

Kumar, Krishna. 1997. *Rebuilding Societies after Civil Wars*. Boulder, Colo.: Lynne Rienner.

Kydd, Andrew, and Barbara F. Walter. 2002. "Sabotaging the Peace: The Politics of Extremist Violence." *International Organization* 56 (2): 263–96.

Lake, Anthony. 2001. *Six Nightmares*. New York: Little Brown.

Lederach, J. P. 2002. "Fostering Effective Reconciliation Processes." In *Forgiveness and Reconciliation: Religion, Public Policy, and Conflict Resolution*, ed. Raymond G. Helmick, S.J., and Rodney L. Peterson. West Conshohocken, Penn.: Templeton Foundation Press.

Licklider, Roy, ed. 1993. *When the Fighting Stops*. New York: New York University Press.

Lindskold, S. 1978. "Trust Development, the GRIT Proposal, and the Effects of Conciliatory Acts on Conflict and Cooperation." *Psychological Bulletin* 85:150–62.

Livingstone D. 2001. "Human Rights: The Challenges and Opportunities for Policing." Paper presented at the Human Rights and Policing Conference, Belfast.

Lyons, Terrence. 2002. "Implementing Peace: The Role of Postsettlement Elections." In *Ending Civil Wars: The Implementation of Peace Agreements,* ed. Stephen John Stedman, Donald Rothchild, and Elizabeth Cousens (pp. 215–35). Boulder, Colo.: Lynne Rienner.

Mac Ginty, R. 2001. "Ethnonational Conflict and Hate Crime." *American Behavioral Scientist* 45 (4): 639–53.

Malan, M. 2000. "Peacebuilding in Southern Africa: Police Reform in Mozambique and South Africa." In *Peace Building and Police Reform,* ed. T. T. Holm and B. B. Eide (pp. 171–90). Portland, Ore.: Cass.

Marshall, Monty G., and Ted Robert Gurr. 2003. *Peace and Conflict 2003: A Global Survey of Armed Conflicts, Self-Determination Movements, and Democracy.* Available online at http://www.cidcm.umd.edu/inscr/index.htm#reports.

Matveeva, A. 2002. "Dagestan: Sustaining a Fragile Peace." In *Searching for Peace in Europe and Eurasia,* ed. P. van Tongeren et al. (pp. 374–88). London: Lynne Rienner.

McIlwaine, C. 1999. "Geography and Development: Violence and Crime as Development Issues." *Progress in Human Geography* 23 (3): 453–63.

Mihajlovic, Dusan. 2002. "Police Reform in Serbia Receives Substantial International Support." In *Serbia 2002.* Belgrade: Ministry for the Protection of Natural Resources and Environment.

Ministry of Internal Affairs. 2000. *Mission and Vision Statement.* Belgrade: Ministry of Internal Affairs.

Mittelman, K., and R. Johnston. 1999. "The Globalization of Organized Crime, the Courtesan State, and the Corruption of Civil Society." *Global Governance* 5: 103–26.

Monk, R. 2001. *Study on Policing in the Federal Republic of Yugoslavia.* Belgrade: Organisation for Security and Co-operation in Europe Mission to the FRY.

Moran, J. 2001. "Democratic Transitions and Forms of Corruption." *Crime, Law and Social Change* 36: 379–93.

Mowday, R. T., R.M. Porter, and L.W. Steers. 1979. "The Measurement of Organizational Commitment." *Journal of Vocational Behavior* 14: 224–47

——. 1982. *Employee-Organization Linkages.* New York: Academic Press.

Naylor, R. T. 1997. "The Rise of the Modern Arms Black Market and the Fall of Supply-Side Control." In *Society under Siege: Crime, Violence, and Illegal Weapon,* ed. V. Gamba. Johannesburg: Halfway House, Institute for Security Studies.

Ohlson, Thomas. 1998. *Power Politics and Peace Policies: Intra-State Conflict Resolution in Southern Africa.* Uppsala, Sweden: University of Uppsala.

Ohlson, Thomas, and John Stephen Stedman. 1994. *The New Is Not Yet Born: Conflict Resolution in Southern Africa.* Washington, D.C.: Brookings.

Ordeshook, Peter C. 1989. *Models of Strategic Choice in Politics.* Ann Arbor: University of Michigan Press.

Organisation for Security and Co-operation in Europe (OSCE). 2002. *Police Reform in Serbia–A Strategic Paper.* Belgrade: Sponsorship Conference.

Osgood, C. E. 1962. *An Alternative to War or Surrender.* Urbana, Ill.: University of Illinois Press.

The Patten Report. 1999. *A New Beginning: Policing in Northern Ireland. The Report of the Independent Commission on Policing for Northern Ireland.* Belfast: Her Majesty's Stationary Office.

Peacock, Susan, and Adriana Beltrán. 2003. *Hidden Powers: Illegal Armed Groups in Post-Conflict Guatemala and the Forces Behind Them.* Washington, D.C.: WOLA.

Pettigrew, Thomas F. 2002. "People Under Threat: Americans, Arabs and Israelis." *Peace and Conflict* 9 (1): 69–90.

Pillar, Paul R. 1983. *Negotiating Peace: War Termination as a Bargaining Process.* Princeton, N.J.: Princeton University Press.

PIOOM (The International Research Program on Causes of Human Rights Violation). 1997. *World Conflict Map.* Leiden, The Netherlands: University of Leiden Press.

Police Authority (Northern Ireland). 1999. *Recorded Crime.* Belfast: Central Statistics Unit.

Police Service of Northern Ireland (PSNI). 2001. *Training Strategy Document.* Belfast: Police Headquarters.

Posen, Barry. 1993. "The Security Dilemma and Ethnic Conflict." *Survival* 35 (1): 104–21. Reprinted in *Ethnic Conflict and International Security,* ed. Michael E. Brown. Princeton, N.J.: Princeton University Press.

Poulton, R. E., and I. Youssouf. 1998. *A Peace of Timbuktu: Democratic Governance, Development and African Peacemaking.* Geneva: UNIDIR.

Pugh, Michael, and Neil Cooper, with Jonathan Goodhand. 2004. *War Economies in Regional Context: The Challenges of Transformation.* Boulder, Colo.: Lynne Rienner.

Rabushka, Alvin, and Kenneth A. Shepsle. 1972. *Politics and Plural Societies: A Theory of Democratic Instability.* Columbus, Ohio: Charles E. Merrill.

Reilly, Ben, and Andrew Reynolds. 2000. "Electoral Systems and Conflict in Divided Societies." In *International Conflict Resolution after the Cold War,* ed. Paul C. Stern and Daniel Druckman (94–108). Washington, D.C.: National Academy Press.

Republic of South Africa. 1998. *Interpellations, Questions and Replies of the National Assembly.* Second Session, Second Parliament. Cape Town: Government Printer.

Robins, P. 2002. "From Small-Time Smuggling to Big-Time Racketeering: Turkey and the Middle East." In *Transnational Organized Crime and International Security: Business as Usual,* ed. M. Berdal and M. Serrano (pp. 141–53). Boulder, Colo.: Lynne Rienner.

Rothchild, Donald. 1997. *Managing Ethnic Conflict in Africa: Pressures and Incentives for Cooperation.* Washington, D.C.: Brookings Institution Press.

Rothchild, Donald, and Alexander L. Groth. 1995. "Pathological Dimensions of Domestic and International Ethnicity." *Political Science Quarterly* 110 (1): 14–82.

Rubin, J. Z, ed. 1981. *Third Party Intervention in Conflict: Kissinger in the Middle East.* New York: Praeger.

Ruffner, K. Conley. 2002. "Colonel Miller and an Army Scandal: The Black Market in Postwar Berlin." *Prologue* 34 (3): 170–83.

Said, Edward. 2000. *The End of the Peace Process.* New York: Pantheon Books.

Saunders, Harold. 1991. "We Need a Larger Theory of Negotiation: The Importance of Prenegotiation." In *Negotiation Theory and Practice,* ed. J. William Breslin and Jeffery Z. Rubin (pp. 57–70). Cambridge, Mass.: The Program on Negotiation at Harvard Law School.

Scarman Commission. 1969. *Disturbances in Northern Ireland.* Belfast: HMSO.

Schelling, Thomas. 1966. *Arms and Influence.* New Haven, Conn.: Yale University Press.

——. 1980. *The Strategy of Conflict.* Cambridge, Mass.: Harvard University Press.

Schirmer, Jennifer. 1998. *The Guatemalan Military Project: A Violence Called Democracy.* Philadelphia: University of Pennsylvania Press.

Schönteich, Martin. 2003. "The White Right: A Threat to South Africa's Internal Security?" *SA Crime Quarterly* (3): 34–48.

Sederberg, Peter C. 1995. "Conciliation as a Counter-Terrorist Strategy." *Journal of Peace Research* 32 (3): 295–312.

Shaw, Mark. 2002. "Crime, Police and Public in Transitional Societies." *Transformation* 49: 1–24.

Sidiropoulos, E. 1998. *South Africa Survey 1997/98.* Johannesburg: South African Institute of Race Relations.

Sieder, Rachel, et al. 2002. *Who Governs? Guatemala Five Years after the Peace Accords.* Cambridge, Mass.: Hemisphere Initiatives.

Sisk, Timothy D. 1993. "The Violence-Negotiation Nexus: South Africa in Transition and the Politics of Uncertainty." *Negotiation Journal* 9: 34–42.

——. 1995. *Democratization in South Africa: The Elusive Social Contract.* Princeton, N.J.: Princeton University Press.

——. 1996. *Power Sharing and International Mediation in Ethnic Conflicts.* New York: Carnegie Commission on Preventing Deadly Conflict, Carnegie Corporation of New York.

Slater, J. 2001. *Assessment Report of the Human Rights, Ethics and Policing Standards in the Federal Republic of Yugoslavia.* Strasbourg, France: Council of Europe.

Spear, Joanna. 2002. "Disarmament and Demobilization." In *Ending Civil Wars: The Implementation of Peace Agreements,* ed. Stephen John Stedman, Donald Rothchild, and Elizabeth Cousens (pp. 141–82). Boulder, Colo.: Lynne Rienner.

Stanley, W., and C. Call. 2003. "Military and Police Reform after Civil Wars." In *Contemporary Peacemaking: Conflict, Violence, and Peace Processes,* ed. John

Darby and Roger MacGinty (pp. 212–23). London and New York: Palgrave-MacMillan.

Stanley, W., and F. Holiday. 2002. "Broad Participation, Diffuse Responsibility: Peace Implementation in Guatemala." In *Ending Civil Wars: The Implementation of Peace Agreements,* ed. Stephen John Stedman, Donald Rothchild, and Elizabeth Cousens (pp. 421–62). Boulder, Colo.: Lynne Rienner.

Stedman, Stephen John. 1996. "Negotiation and Mediation in Internal Conflict." In *The International Dimensions of Internal Conflict,* ed. M.E. Brown (pp. 341–76). Cambridge, Mass. and London: MIT Press.

——. 1997. "Spoiler Problems in Peace Processes." *International Security* 22 (2): 5–53.

——. 2001. *Implementing Peace Agreements in Civil Wars: Lessons and Recommendations for Policymakers.* IPA Policy Paper on Peace Implementation. New York: International Peace Academy.

——. 2002. "Policy Implications." In *Ending Civil Wars: The Implementation of Peace Agreements,* ed. Stephen John Stedman, Donald Rothchild, and Elizabeth M. Cousens (pp. 663–71). Boulder, Colo.: Lynne Rienner.

——. 2003. "Peace Processes and the Challenges of Violence." In *Contemporary Peacemaking: Conflict, Violence, and Peace Processes,* ed. John Darby and Roger Mac Ginty (103–13). London and New York: Palgrave-MacMillan.

Stedman, Stephen John, and Donald Rothchild. 1996. "Peace Operations: From Short-Term to Long-Term Commitment." *International Peacekeeping* 3 (2): 27–44.

Stedman, Stephen John, Donald Rothchild, and Elizabeth M. Cousens, eds. 2002. *Ending Civil Wars: The Implementation of Peace Agreements.* Boulder, Colo.: Lynne Rienner.

Suhrke, Astri, and Howard Adelman. 1999. *The Path of Genocide: The Rwanda Crisis from Uganda to Zaire.* New Brunswick, N.J.: Transaction.

Taylor, Maxwell. 1991. *The Fanatics: A Behavioral Approach to Political Violence.* London: Brassey's.

Taylor, Rupert. 2002. "Justice Denied: Political Violence in KwaZulu-Natal after 1994." Violence and Transition Series, vol. 6. Johannesburg: Centre for the Study of Violence and Reconciliation.

Trivunovich, Marijana. 2003. *Managing Police Reform.* Budapest: Open Society Institute.

United Nations Children's Fund (UNICEF). 1997. *Human Development Report: Globalization with a Human Face.* New York: United Nations

——. 2002. *Human Development Report: Deepening Democracy in a Fragmented World.* New York: United Nations.

United Nations Development Program (UNDP). 1994. *New Dimensions on Human Security.* New York, United Nations.

United Nations Institute for Disarmament Research (UNIDIR). 1996–98. *The Disarmament and Conflict Resolution (DRC) Series.* Geneva: UNIDIR.

Van Zyl Smit, D. 1999. "Criminological Ideas and the South Africa Transition." *British Journal of Criminology* 39 (2): 198–215.

Vickers, G. 1999. "Renegotiating Internal Security: The Lessons of Central America." In *Comparative Peace Processes in Latin America,* ed. C. Arnson (pp. 389–413). Stanford, Calif.: Stanford University Press.

Wagner, Robert Harrison. 1993. "The Causes of Peace." In *Stopping the Killing,* ed Roy Licklider. New York: New York University Press.

Wallensteen, P., and M. Sollenberg. 2000. "Armed Conflict, 1989–99." *Journal of Peace Research* 37 (5): 635–49.

——. 2001. "Armed Conflict, 1989–2000." *Journal of Peace Research* 38 (5): 629–44.

Walter, Barbara F. 1997. "The Critical Barrier to Civil War Settlement." *International Organization* 51 (3): 336–64.

——. 1998. "Designing Transitions from Violent Civil War." IGCC Policy Paper 31. San Diego: UC Institute on Global Conflict and Cooperation. Available online at http://www-igcc.ucsd.edu/igcc2/PolicyPapers/pp31.html.

——. 2002. *Committing to Peace: The Successful Resolution Settlement of Civil Wars.* Princeton, N.J.: Princeton University Press.

Wantchekon, Leonard. 1999. "On the Nature of First Democratic Elections." *Journal of Conflict Resolution* 43 (2): 245–58.

Wood, Elisabeth Jean. 1999. "Civil War Settlement: Modeling the Bases of Compromise." Paper presented to the Annual Meeting of the American Political Science Association, Atlanta.

Zahar, Marie-Jöelle. 2000. "Fanatics, Mercenaries, Brigands and Politicians: Militia Decision-Making and Conflict Resolution." PhD diss., McGill University.

——. 2003. "Reframing the Spoiler Debate in Peace Processes." In *Contemporary Peacemaking: Conflict, Violence, and Peace Processes,* ed. John Darby and Roger MacGinty. London and New York: Palgrave-MacMillan.

Zartman, I. William, ed. 1980. *The Study of Elites in the Middle East.* New York: Praeger.

——. 1989a. "Prenegotiation: Phases and Functions." In *Getting to the Table: The Processes of International Prenegotiation,* ed. Janice Gross Stein (pp. 237–53). Baltimore, Md.: John Hopkins University Press.

——. 1989b. *Ripe for Resolution: Conflict and Intervention in Africa.* New Haven, Conn.: Yale University Press.

——, ed. 1995. *Elusive Peace: Negotiating an End to Civil Wars.* Washington, D.C.: Brookings Institution.

——. 1997. "Explaining Oslo." *International Negotiations* (11) 2: 195–215.

——. 2000. "Ripeness: The Hurting Stalemate and Beyond." In *International Conflict Resolution after the Cold War,* ed. Paul C. Stern and Daniel Druckman (225–50). Washington, D.C.: National Academy Press.

Zartman, I. William, and Katarina Vogeli. 2000. "Prevention Gained, Prevention Lost: Collapse, Competition and Coup in Congo." In *Opportunities Missed, Opportunities Gained,* ed. Bruce Jentleson. Lanham, Md.: Rowman and Littlefield.

Additional Works Consulted

Amnesty International. Various Years. *Annual Reports.* Available online at http://web.amnesty.org/library/index/ENGEUR450162002.

Babovic, B. 2000. "Of Control and Oversight of the Police in Yugoslavia." In *Civilian Control of the Army and Police,* compiled by M. Hadsic. Belgrade: Media Centre and Centre for Civil-Military Relations.

Caparini, M. 2002. *Human Rights and Yugoslav Legislation on the Security Sector in Compendium of Yugoslav Laws on the Security Sector: Human Rights and Democratic Oversight Aspects.* Belgrade: Geneva Centre for the Democratic Control of Armed Forces and the Centre for Civil-Military Relations.

Dunn, S., D. Murray, and D. Walsh. 2002. *Cross-Border Police Co-operation in Ireland.* Limerick: University of Limerick.

Falk, Richard. 2003. *The Great Terror War.* New York: Olive Branch Press.

Frost, B. 1998. *Struggling to Forgive: Nelson Mandela and South Africa's Search for Reconciliation.* London: Harper Collins.

Gamba, V. 1997. *Society under Siege: Crime, Violence and Illegal Weapons.* Johannesburg: Halfway House, Institute for Security Studies.

Glenny, M. 1996. *The Fall of Yugoslavia.* London: Penguin

Hadsic, M., comp. 2000. *Civilian Control of the Army and Police.* Belgrade: Media Centre and Centre for Civil-Military Relations.

Human Rights Watch. Various Years. *Annual Reports.* Available online at http://www.hrw.org/campaigns/september11/opportunismwatch.htm.

Miall, Hugh, Oliver Ramsbotham, and Tom Woodhouse. 1998. *Contemporary Conflict Resolution.* London: Macmillan.

Organisation for Security and Co-operation in Europe (OSCE). 2002. *Project Proposals for Police Reform, Republic of Serbia.* Belgrade: Sponsorship Conference.

Ryder, C. 2000. *A Force Under Fire.* London: Arrow Books.

Saferafrica. 2003. *Report of the AU-NEPAD Consultations on Peace and Security.* Pretoria: Saferafrica.

Shaw, Mark. 2002. *Crime and Policing in Post-Apartheid South Africa: Transforming Under Fire.* Cape Town and Johannesburg: David Philip Publisher.

Stern, Paul C., and Daniel Druckman, eds. 2000. *International Conflict Resolution after the Cold War.* Washington, D.C.: National Academy Press.

About the Contributors

JOHN DARBY is professor of comparative ethnic studies at the Kroc Institute at the University of Notre Dame, where he is director of the Research Initiative for the Resolution of Ethnic Conflict (RIREC). Darby has written or edited eleven books and more than one hundred other academic publications, mostly dealing with ethnic conflict internationally. Recent publications include *The Effects of Violence on Peace Processes* (United States Institute of Peace, 2001); and *Contemporary Peacemaking*, edited with Roger Mac Ginty (Palgrave/Macmillan, 2003).

CHRISTINE HÖGLUND is assistant professor at the Department of Peace and Conflict Research, Uppsala University. Her research and publications cover the relationship between violence and peace processes, including her PhD thesis, *Violence in the Midst of Peace Negotiations: Cases from Guatemala, Northern Ireland, South Africa and Sri Lanka.*

VIRGINIA GAMBA is director of SaferAfrica, South Africa. She works extensively on peace and security issues in Africa facilitating policy, legislation, and operative implementation of national and regional plans for sustainable peace, disarmament, and development processes in Africa.

ROGER MAC GINTY is a lecturer in politics at the University of York. He is the editor and author (with John Darby) of a number of books on conflict management, including *The Management of Peace Processes* (Macmillan/St. Martins, 2000).

DOMINIC MURRAY is professor of peace studies and director of the Centre for Peace and Development Studies at the University of Limerick. He is the author of *Worlds Apart: Segregated Schooling in Northern Ireland* (Belfast: Appletree Press, 1985) and *Cross-Border Police Co-operation in Ireland* (Belfast: Appletree Press, 2002).

TIMOTHY SISK is associate professor and director of the Bachelor of Arts Program in International Studies at the University of Denver, Colorado. He is the author of *Democracy at the Local Level: The International IDEA Handbook on Representation, Participation, and Conflict Management and Governance* (Stockholm: Institute for Democracy and Election Assistance, 2001).

MARIE-JÖELLE ZAHAR is assistant professor of political science at the Universite de Montreal. She works on nonstate actors in civil wars with a regional interest in the Balkans and the Middle East. She is currently working on a book, *Militia Institutions and Vulnerability: The Domestic Politics of Civil Conflict Resolution.*

I. WILLIAM ZARTMAN is the Jacob Blaustein Distinguished Professor of International Organization and Conflict Management and director of the Conflict Management Program at the Johns Hopkins University School of Advanced International Studies. He has a PhD from Yale and an honorary doctorate from the Catholic University of Louvain. He is the author of *Ripe for Resolution* (Oxford University Press, 1989) and editor/co-author of *Preventive Negotiations* (Rowman and Littlefield, 2001) and *Peacemaking in International Conflicts* (United States Institute of Peace, 1997, 2002), among others.